BOYLE CO PUBLIC LIBRARY

3 6402 10057069 7

W9-ADL-687

Boyle County Public Libra.

The Perception of the Unborn Across the Cultures of the World

To the memory of A. Ferdinand Engel
without whose loving encouragement
this book would have never been finished.

Walburga von Raffler-Engel

The Perception of the Unborn Across the Cultures of the World

Hogrefe & Huber Publishers
Seattle · Toronto · Bern · Göttingen

Library of Congress Cataloging-in-Publication Data

is available via the Library of Congress Marc Database under
LC Catalog Card Number 93-061410

Canadian Cataloguing in Publication Data

Von Raffler-Engel, Walburga, 1920–
    The perception of the unborn across the cultures of the world

Includes bibliographical references and index.
ISBN 0-88937-120-2

28N

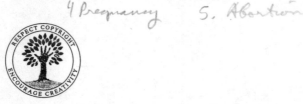

1. Fetus – Cross-cultural studies. 2. Prenatal care – Cross-cultural
studies. 3. Prenatal influences – Cross-cultural studies. I. Title.
RG600.V65   1993   618.2'4   C93-095307-X

4 Pregnancy   5. Abortion

Copyright © 1994 by Hogrefe & Huber Publishers

P. O. Box 2487, Kirkland, WA 98083-2487
12–14 Bruce Park Ave., Toronto, Ontario M4P 2S3

No part of this book may be reproduced, stored in a retrieval system or by any means, electronic, mechanical, photocopying, mi-
crofilming, recording or otherwise, without the written permission from the publisher.

Printed in USA

ISBN 0-88937-120-2
Hogrefe & Huber Publishers, Seattle Toronto Bern Göttingen

ISBN 3-8017-0728-8
Hogrefe & Huber Publishers, Göttingen Bern Seattle Toronto

Table of Contents

Chapter 7: Our Individual Personality is Formed Before Birth 129

Chapter 8: Enculturation Begins Before Birth . 141

Introduction

When people pick up this book and see its title associated with my name, they may wonder why a professor of linguistics would write about prenatal care. But they will not be puzzled for long as they realize that linguistics is the study of language.

A basic purpose of language is communication and only a healthy and intelligent individual possesses the power to communicate effectively. To adequately express oneself and to understand clearly what our interlocutor intends to tell us is no easy feat. It is not enough to know the vocabulary and the grammar of the spoken medium and to be able to master the fine art of facial expression and body movement. One must also be sensitive to the nuances of the tone of voice and grasp their meaning in the speaker's culture. In order to sustain a conversation the speakers must know the rules the culture prescribes for such interaction.

All parents want their children to grow up and become happy, self-supporting adults. They know that for a satisfying personal life as well as a successful career it is necessary to master the art of social interaction. I wanted to know what parents in all parts of the world do about teaching their children to become good communicators. I also wanted to know how early the teaching process begins. Here I will present what I found out about the very earliest period. I have been quite patient in my pursuit and this book has been in the making for a long time.

Some thirty years ago, I was writing a book on how children communicate during their first year of life, before they develop formal language (von Raffler-Engel 1964). In my research I discovered that they communicate quite successfully and that they do so as soon as they are born. This made me think that, if they communicate so well as soon as they come out of the womb, they must have had some previous learning experience. They must have communicated while they were still inside the womb (Ibid., p. 75). Thus, I decided to research the behavior of the unborn. I was then the mother of two small children and I vividly recollected that I frankly did not speak to them much differently before and after their birth. I also was quite conscious that they responded to me when I caressed my abdomen. Often, when I discontinued caressing, they started kicking like they were demanding more attention. Evidently, their tactic worked because I resumed the caressing motion.

At that time I was a visiting professor at the University of Florence in Italy and I started interviewing mothers and mothers-to-be in that city and the surrounding countryside. All the women agreed that there is communication between the mother and the child she is carrying.

With sincere affection I remember the late Professor Giacomo Devoto who in 1963 organized my first lecture on this subject at the Linguistic Circle of the University of Florence, Italy. I have since then presented other lectures on my favorite research topic at the Linguistic Circle whenever I came to Florence over the years. The response from the audience was always stimulating.

I returned to the University of Florence for a semester in 1986 as visiting professor in the Department of Psychology to give a course and some lectures on prenatal development. My students and colleagues were extremely stimulating and I am sincerely grateful to Professor Francesca Morino Abbele who obtained the funding from the Italian National Science Foundation.

When I returned to a regular position as professor of Linguistics in the United States of America, I continued interviewing mothers and now also fathers in Nashville, Tennessee, where I was living. In America, much more than in Italy, my idea of a lively interaction between the mother and her unborn child seemed far-fetched to many people. Many publishers thought that the subject matter would not be of any interest to the American public. The exception was Professor Joshua Fishman, who at the time, was the editor of the *International Journal of the Sociology of Language*. He asked me to prepare a special issue on my findings. But I was unable to secure sufficient time away from my teaching duties at Vanderbilt University to complete my research for such a monograph. The university, at that time, was not interested in research across different cultures, be it about the living or the yet to be born.

It was generally an exhilarating experience to talk to women about the life of the unborn child, but I almost cried when talking to women in the People's Republic of China where I spent a summer as a visiting professor. In the back of their mind was the thought of forced abortion. Only a handful of men and women approved of it as a necessary intervention to keep their country from becoming overpopulated. Most associated it with infanticide imposed on them against their will.

Without funding it was not possible to produce videotapes, as I had wished to do. The only video which I was able to produce came about because one year in the course I taught on nonverbal communication, I had a number of students from the School of Nursing. I assigned them to go to the waiting room of a prenatal clinic and videotape the women who were sitting there waiting for their turn. The results were striking. On the screen all of these women are seen stroking their abdomen, with their face turned downward toward their belly. They did not speak except to each other, but it was apparent from the movements of their hands and the direction of their head when not speaking to another woman that they communicated with the child they were carrying.

During one of my lecture tours in Germany, I viewed a birthing film at the Max Planck Institute near Munich. This film of a normal delivery showed the emerging infant reacting in a totally different manner to the touch of his mother than to that of the obstetrician. The baby arched his back as if in protest, but was calmed by the touch of his mother. It became apparent that he must have recognized the touch of his mother from when she caressed her abdomen during pregnancy (von Raffler-Engel 1988 a). Some years later I mentioned this observation of mine to Ms. Sue Reynolds, a mother of one, who was interested in learning about my project. This woman told me she could think of her own delivery where her daughter seemed to react negatively to the touch of the doctor. After birth, when the attending nurse placed the baby on her mother's belly, she had the feeling that the newborn still registered her dismay by pushing her lower lip out. Eventually the mother stroked the back of the baby who then relaxed comfortably.

Viewing a delivery on film — or experiencing one's own — makes it clear that a pregnant woman needs to touch her abdomen and speak to the child she is carrying so that during its birthing experience the child will feel reassured by a familiar touch and known voice. Eastern women do this consciously with the purpose of creating a familiar ambience for the child and to lay the ground-work for easing the hardship of having to learn so many things later in life.

In the West the spread of the practice of intentional communica-tion with the unborn started somewhat later but as medical science advances, more and more attention is paid to the interactive needs of the unborn. Even as recently as the early nineties, many people were surprised when I told them that it has been documented that when two women speak at the same time, a newborn will turn its head toward its mother (von Raffler-Engel 1983, 1988).

The Japanese language has a word for the proper care of the unborn: *taikyó*. The Japanese dictionary definitions of this word are as follows: "Education for unborn children. A woman should try to sit straight, to have a correct diet, to see no evil, to listen to good music and suitable counsel in order for her to provide a good influence for her unborn child." (Daikanwa Jiten Showa 61, vol. 13, p. 9628); "During her pregnancy a pregnant woman maintains her mental and emotional calmness and trains herself to behave better so that she can provide a favorable influence for her unborn child." (Nihon Kokuga Daijiten, Showa 49, vol. 12, p. 529)

Beyond the dictionary definition of *taikyó*, what fascinates me about this word is its written composition. It consists of the kangi characters for *teaching* and *womb*. The two characters were al-ready combined in China and the Daikanwa dictionary as an ex-ample gives the story of the Chinese empress Tai-zan who lived in the 13th century B. C. and who "commenced the instruction of her child when he was still in her womb." (Stucken 1907, p. 199) Tai-zan actually had the sages of her court instruct her child as if it had already been born and could hear and understand. I talked with Chinese friends of mine and it appears that the concept of teaching/womb is identical to the Japanese one, as defined by the Japanese dictionaries quoted above.

In present day Japan there is more to *taikyó* than the obligation of the mother to control her behavior for the benefit of the child she is carrying. She will play music not only for her own enjoyment which is hormonally transmitted to the child. She will play music for the fetus to hear it directly and she knows that playing the same tune later on during delivery will calm the emerging child and that once born the child will recognize the tune and favor it compared to music that may be equally pleasant but that it has not heard before. Pregnant women will read aloud convinced that the child in their womb, even though it does not understand the exact words, will start getting used to being read to after birth during its childhood when being read to and reading by itself will become an important part of its formal education.

I am told that this custom originated some twenty years ago. It is my opinion that this is not a new custom, but the revival of a very old one. The collection of folktales from around the world which I have assembled, in my opinion, testify to the old practice of teaching the child in the womb by appealing directly to it in addition to the indirect hormonal transmission of the mother's calm emotional state. All cultures, throughout history, emphasize emotional well being in addition to the pregnant woman being properly cared for as to physical health.

As a linguist, I am very much interested in what goes on in reading and speaking to the unborn. As language is bi-modal, verbal and nonverbal, I also attribute great importance to the caressing of the swelling abdomen. Presently, besides mothers, fathers are getting more and more involved in communicating with their offspring before it is born.

It is the concept of *taikyó* that will constitute the essence of this book. I have practiced this concept since I had my first child, in the late fifties, and studied it ever since. But I had no real word for it until my good friend Prof. Keiko Ikegami mentioned it to me in Tokyo. I have spoken with many women from other cultures who practice the concept but have no word for it. It is, of course, possible that there are languages with such a word and I just do not happen to know about them.

I wanted to explore the life of the unborn and my chance to give it my full attention came once I was able to retire from most of my university duties. This book is the result of what I have found out so far. I could have gone on forever, but I prefer to close at a certain moment in time in order to share my findings with my readers. I wanted to cover as many nations as possible and include all social classes.

College students are easily available, the adult middle and upper classes can also be reached fairly well. It is not so easy to reach the working classes. This is particularly true in the United States of America where many have great difficulty reading questionnaires and even more difficulties in writing answers to them. They have to be contacted one by one on a personal basis. In order to gain access to blue collar workers I took a brief stint of employment in a factory. To reach construction workers I climbed ladders and walked over cement blocks and mud holes. I wanted to talk with farmers, but driving into the countryside was simply too time-consuming.

This is not a statistically perfect piece of research but it provides novel information from around the world and its hope is to be of help to make the period of gestation even more heart-warming than it already is. And maybe it will also be helpful to the little one yet unborn by drawing attention to its needs for those who are not yet practicing *taikyó*. I am convinced that the mother's interaction with the child she carries will affect its intelligence. From my survey it appears that many women are skeptical about this and I hope this book will convince them otherwise. I hope I no longer will encounter a young woman saying that if she were overheard speaking to her unborn child, she'd be embarrassed and "feel foolish."

To accomplish my research about the perception of the unborn in diverse cultures I started out preparing a questionnaire with a number of closed questions and a modicum of open questions. Without disturbing the basic unity of the responses I made the necessary superficial changes according to whether the questionnaire was destined for mothers, fathers, students, or theologians. The set of my questionnaires is in the appendix.

My research methodology is a combination of the two classical methods practiced by sociologists. (A brief presentation of the pros and cons of these two systems can be found in a debate of the American Social Science Research Council, see Anonymous 1987). One method is streamlined and forces the interviewee to give an answer to the question as formulated by the interviewer. It does not leave much leeway to express additional ideas, but it has the clear advantage that the answers can be tabulated and comparisons between different cultures and religions are easily drawn.

The second approach, termed the method of "interviews as discourse," allows for the free flow of conversation and brings out much unexpected novel information. In the oral interview pauses and hesitancies are recorded and the interviewee is never pressed for time. In my methodology I hope that I got a good picture of what the interviewee freely thought and that I gained all the information he or she wanted to convey without losing the advantage of compatible data which could be properly tabulated. No survey is perfect, but I have carefully tried to avoid loaded questions.

By far the majority of interviews were conducted orally. I made certain that the questions had all been memorized, but I also made sure that the conversation would flow freely by posing these questions in whichever order was best suited within the framework of each informal interviewing session. Incidentally, this is something that all people have in common, they will open up to a friendly interlocutor and they will volunteer information they would not be likely to share with somebody who treats them coolly like standard research subjects.

Several hundred people were interviewed and many of the interviews lasted for more than one hour. Most of the person-to-person interviews were conducted by my son, Robert Engel, who was trained as a professional journalist. He started doing this to help me but gradually became fascinated with the subject matter in its own right. It became clear to me that men can get as much involved as women in looking at the future generation. My son conducted an interview even when he was on a business trip in Ireland.

Much appreciation goes to my husband, A. Ferdinand Engel, a specialist in international affairs with the U.S. Department of State and later director of an inter-cultural organization, who greatly helped me in tracing people with information that might be relevant to my project. He shared my love for this work, but sadly died before its completion. He gave more time than anybody else to this project of mine.

While I was working on this book over such an extensive period, as I went along, I presented some of my findings at meetings of learned societies, especially the Language Origins Society, the NATO Institute for Advanced Studies, the European Sociobiological Society and the Social Science Research Council of UNESCO. I am grateful for the constructive comments made by my colleagues at those times.

Many former students and personal friends of mine offered their assistance gathering the data I needed for this book. It would be a long list indeed and I am deeply grateful to all of them. They did not wish their names to be listed individually. Only one among the many who helped me out of interest in my project expressed the desire that her name be listed in this thank-you note of mine: Ms. Sue Reynolds, coordinator of bilingual education in the Nashville school system. At my suggestion she was kind enough to drive up once to the Tennessee hills to look for superstitions. I asked her to drive to the hills because some of my students had told me that these hills harbor many super-stitions. Ms. Reynolds started out looking for a "witch" but was unable to contact her and so she interviewed other residents for me. Ms. Reynolds also interviewed some local refugees according to my questionnaires.

In addition to collecting data from interviews, I went through the literature dealing with the perception of the unborn from an-tiquity to the present time. This extensive reading could not have been accomplished without the competent and cordial assistance of Ms. Anne Reuland, reference librarian at the Central Library of Vanderbilt University. Ms. Reuland prepared all the computer searches on the various aspects of my research and then located the relevant articles and books either in our library or through inter-library loan. She made many useful suggestions and I am deeply indebted to her. I am also indebted to my Japanese editor, Ms. Hidako Mikada, who provided me with several useful sources of reference.

To provide the scientific basis for my assertion that the child is capable of communicating before it is born, I consulted medical texts on the sensory capabilities of the fetus. Ms. Byrd S. Helguera, associate director for the Vanderbilt University Medical Center Li-brary was most helpful and extremely generous of her time in pro-viding me with the relevant materials. I updated the published in-formation through conversations with the medical faculty and I also spoke with nurses in the maternity section. I am thankful to all who so generously gave of their time and knowledge.

I also want to express my gratitude to my typist, Ms. Arliene Dearing, who patiently retyped many revisions and additions. Much appreciation also goes to Mark Sutterfield of Hogrefe and Huber, who kept encouraging me, and to my editor Dr. Thomas

Tebaz for suggesting that I write a more extensive book than I had originally planned.

How powerful the brain of the unborn child is will become ever more apparent as medical science progresses. And in its progress it confirms what tradition knew long ago. The fetus is not a passive appendix of its mother's body. It is a human being in its early stages of development. Recent findings at the Cornell Laboratory for Pregnancy and Newborn Research show that in unborn sheep (whose reproductive system is similar to humans) the onset of labor is triggered by a brain signal that releases the hormones that initiate the series of reactions necessary for birth. The director of the Laboratory comments that it makes sense that the fetus control the timing of birth because it is the brain of the fetus which can determine when the fetal organs are ready for life outside the womb (McDonald and Nathanielsz 1991).

The human newborn cannot survive without a caretaker during the first two years of life. Babies whose physical needs are provided for, but who are not given emotional support and spoken to, will have a slower than normal rate of development and many will die. In the same orphanages those babies who get special attention from an attendant will prosper. The need to communicate is as basic as any other requirement of the human condition. As such it begins in utero.

The power to communicate, in its bi-modal verbal and nonverbal manifestation, develops from the embryonic stage on, like all other mental and physical attributes of the human being (von Raffler-Engel 1991 a). Birth is an important event, but not one that radically alters the gradual maturation of the communicative system, from kicking, to crying, to pointing, to the melodic variations of the carrier sound, to the articulated variations of the holophrastic word, to language (von Raffler-Engel 1964). The beginning is conception as the brain starts to develop from then on. The power to communicate terminates when the brain ceases to function through death or disease. Death of a fetus comes from miscarriage or abortion. Disease and abnormalities are of many shapes.

For millennia folktales have elaborated on the communicative capabilities of the child in its mother's womb. The interviews with people of many cultures revealed a richness of variations on the one common theme of the fetus talking to its mother and to others in the outside world. I am convinced that if I had traveled further and interviewed an even larger number of people, I would have found more variations on this all-human theme. Books on famous people, especially heroes and saints also provided stories on this topic from antiquity to the present day.

The collection of the stories I am presenting here to the readers could be titled "Superstitions — but are they?" Of course, I do not believe that a fetus can speak in adult language and audibly from the inside of the womb, but what is so relevant about these stories is that the folk wisdom has preserved the idea that the unborn has a personality in its own right and that it is sensitive to joy and pain. What is most noticeable is that the legends about unborn children communicating from inside the womb can be found in all parts of the world and throughout the centuries. When people became strictly science oriented, they dismissed these "old wives' tales" and no longer considered them allegorical elaborations of a real fact. It is only now that medical evidence has lent luster to the traditions of fetal intelligence.

If the reader asks why in this book the stories of old do not precede the chapter on the recent scientific discoveries, I will answer that in our skeptical age we would not appreciate the old legends had we not previously been shown that they do have purpose. The pregnant woman must listen to the baby inside her and she should encourage its father to share with her the education of their child. He can play music and also sing and he can put his hand on his wife's abdomen and feel the baby kicking. The second and the third chapter, albeit written from a very different perspective, in reality bring out the same truth.

The chapter following the one on superstitions surrounding pregnancy recounts of the fertility rites that have been practiced from time immemorial. We now have medically tested fertility drugs. Before that time infertile couples used magic and other so-called unscientific methods to insure the continuation of their families. The need was the same, the belief in a possible cure was equally powerful, only the methods differed. Medicine has become more effective, but it is always elaborating on an old theme.

Soon medical research will bring about a breakthrough in allowing couples to determine the sex of the child they will procreate by calculating certain days in relation to the menstrual period of the woman. Folk beliefs abound on how to secure the birth of a son and here it is hard to speak of the wisdom of old traditions because the advice proffered to prospective parents is often quite absurd. The one advice that makes sense is given to the Jews who are allowed to pray for a son until the wife is pregnant, but not after she has conceived because at that time the sex of the child has been decided and it is not lawful to ask God for something that goes counter to the rules of nature. I said "to pray for a son." It is the desire for a male child that appears to be universal.

Through amniocentesis we can now detect the sex of a fetus. People have always been curious about whether they are going to become the parents of a boy or girl. Before amniocentesis people used to guess with ineffective, but luckily quite harmless, devices or by simply looking at the mother's face or at her abdomen. The fifth chapter of my book will report on the superstitious practices to secure a son as well as of the attempts to detect the sex of the child a woman is carrying.

While I was researching the capabilities of the unborn child and its perception in various places of the world, I was reminded that life and personhood are not synonymous. It is clear that life begins at conception. When personhood begins is a far more controversial issue. It may begin at three months of gestational age, or when the fetus reaches viability, between six and seven months, or at birth, or at three days or one month after birth. On the island of Okinawa, I was told, a child is considered a person only when it reaches twelve years of age. When death occurs, it is only after that age that there will be a traditional burial.

For a linguist, most interesting is the attitude of the Mayan Indians in Guatemala. There, when a women is asked how many children she has, she will give the number of all the children she conceived, including miscarriages and children that died in infancy. The watershed for a child is not its birth but the moment when it can speak in regular sentences. A child becomes a person when it can talk like an adult, such as replying to a question with a complete answer like "Yes, I want to eat."

When the child can speak, it will be named. Before that time all children are called "Monkey," which implies they are not yet considered fully human. If a child dies before it can speak, it will not be accorded a regular funeral. Like a miscarriage it is simply buried in the ground. The pregnant woman is well taken care of and given massages throughout her pregnancy. Should she die during delivery, she will go to heaven and her baby will nurse forever. Nobody else is so lucky to go to heaven after death. All other persons go to a sad place.

An impending birth is never mentioned by a woman and neighbors are not allowed to look at the newborn. For the first two years of life, the Mayan mothers carry their babies on the back and during that period infants are discouraged from attempting to walk. Before the child can speak clearly, it is looked at as if it were still inside the womb. The mother's back is considered the equivalent of the womb for the period after birth and before the onset of full language.

As language is so important, nobody speaks in baby talk to an infant. Everybody speaks in adult language and even a very small child is constantly corrected. I am told, however, that Mayan mothers do not consciously communicate with the unborn (the information about the Mayan Indians was given to me in a personal communication by Dr. Duncan M. Earle, assistant professor of anthropology at Texas A&M University who is a specialist on the Indians of Guatemala).

The different perceptions of when personhood begins in the human being which I noticed in my interviews and when going through the literature brought to mind the need to know more about how the religions of the world view the unborn. The diverse practices of burial rites for miscarriages and small infants are closely associated with religion. To explore this association, it became necessary to contact representatives of the major religions. My journalist son did most of these interviews and the religious leaders were extremely generous in giving me their time and undivided attention. Chapter six will report on the burial rites of different cultures.

While the second chapter of this book presents hard scientific evidence that the child can learn before it is born, the following chapters deal with folk beliefs, legends and religious practices. These are followed by chapters describing my empirical research on how the child becomes a member of its culture before it is born and how its individual personality develops during its intrauterine period of life. The last chapter will again be in the medical field. It will present the advice from an experienced obstetrician/gynecologist who is also a firm believer in the interactive needs of the fetus. Dr. M. Houston Sarratt received his medical degree from the Vanderbilt University School of Medicine in 1947 and has been in practice since 1952.

Most of my research is empirical, but the book has two chapters that are so exclusively. One is the chapter on the early enculturation of the child. It is based on my observations over the years living in various countries.

The other chapter deals with the correlation of the prenatal and the postnatal behavior of the human being. It is entirely based on my interviews with women that have borne more than one child. In a certain sense, this chapter provides the most convincing evidence for the basic tenet of this book.

In the appendix the reader will find a summary of the salient points of fetal development (von Raffler-Engel 1991 b). Some of human behavior is instinctive and some is learned. Learning begins while the child is still in its mother's womb. The child's learning process is continuous, but there is a difference in the learning environment before birth and after birth. One can therefore speak of two phases of learning, the prenatal and the postnatal.

This book is concerned with the prenatal phase of learning and consequently the prenatal phase of teaching on the part of the parents. At about three months of gestational age, mothers observe that their child starts kicking. In reality, of course, the fetus has been moving all along, but it is only after this period that the mother can clearly feel the kicking and even a third party can hold his/her hand on the mother's abdomen and feel the pushing motion beneath the skin. Later, little bulges become visible when the baby pushes its arms or its feet against the wall of the uterus. Many women have told me that the baby kicks as a signal to the mother, to tell her "I am here."

"I am here and I need care" is what this book wants to convey to the reader. It hopes to encourage pregnant women and their entire families to practice *taikyó* in the extended meaning of this word. From embryo, to fetus, to baby, to infant, a child needs to grow mentally as well as physically. It is the parents' responsibility to facilitate this growth. If reading this book will have contributed just a little to make the task of *taikyó* even more joyful than it already is, I will feel gratified.

This book is by no means an exhaustive source of information. What it hopes to accomplish is to stimulate concern for the unborn on the part of everybody. It also hopes to stimulate further research on the part of the professional scholars, beyond those working in the medical sciences. If I have time, I may write a sequel to this book. There are many more folk beliefs to be brought out through the method of oral history. I hope to collect the wisdom of old before it will be forgotten.

I know that we are all pressed for time and also that our interests vary. To make my material accessible to the hurried reader of the nineties, each chapter has been written like a self-contained unit. It is also not necessary to adhere to the sequence of the chapters. Of course, I hope that my readers will be stimulated to cover the entire book, but this is not essential for an understanding of each of the topics I have covered. The subject index should be of assistance to those of my readers who are interested in varied aspects of areas that have been dealt with in more than one section of the book.

No topic has been treated exhaustively for lack of time and funding, but I hope to have stimulated enough interest so that some colleague may eventually write a comprehensive treatment of one or the other of my topics.

References

Anonymous (1987). The role of the interviewer in survey measurements. *Current Activities of the Council (Social Science Research Council)*, 41 (1/2), 48–52.

Daikanwa Jiten Showa 61 (3rd ed.). Showa 33 (1st ed.). Tokyo: Taishukan

McDonald, T. & Nathanielsz, P. (1991). Bilateral destruction of the fetal paraventricular nuclei prolongs gestation in sheep. *American Journal of Obstetrics and Gynecology, 165*, 764–770.

Nihon Kokuga Daijiten Showa 49. Tokyo: Shogakkan.

Stucken, E. (1907). *Astralmythen* (5 vols. in 1 vol.). Leipzig: Eduard Pfeiffer

von Raffler-Engel, W. (1964). *Il prelinguaggio infantile*. Brescia: Paideia (Studi grammaticali e Linguistici 7).

von Raffler-Engel, W. (1980). Development kinesics: The acquisition of nonverbal conversational behavior. In W. von Raffler-Engel (Ed.), *Aspects of nonverbal behavior* (pp. 133–159). Lisse: Swets & Zeitlinger.

von Raffler-Engel, W. (1983). On the synchronous development of gesticulation and vocalization in man's early communicative behavior. In E. de Grolier (Ed.), *Glossogenetics; The origin and evolution of language* (pp. 295–312) (Proceedings of the Transdisciplinary Symposium on

Glossogenetics, Paris, UNESCO 1981). Paris: Harwood Academic Publishers.

von Raffler-Engel, W. (1988). The impact of covert factors in cross-cultural communication. In F. Poyatos (Ed.), *Cross-cultural perspectives in nonverbal communication* (pp. 71–104). Toronto: C.J. Hogrefe.

von Raffler-Engel, W. (1991 a). The contribution of psycholinguistics to the study of language origins. In J. Wind, B. Chiarelli, B. Bichakjian & A. Nocentini (Eds.), *Language origin: A multi-disciplinary approach* (pp. 183–193) (Based on the NATO Advanced Study Institute held in Cortona, Italy. July 8–22, 1988). Dordrecht: Kluwer Academic Publishers.

von Raffler-Engel, W. (1991 b). *The perception of the unborn across cultures and religions*. Abstract available at the Third International Conference on Cross-Cultural Communication: East and West, Tainan, Taiwan, Chen Kung University, April 1–7.

Questionnaire for College Students

Name . . . . Sex: M ☐   F ☐
undergrad. ☐ graduate ☐ professional ☐
Country of origin and place of birth: . . . .
Date of birth: . . . . Marital Status: . . . .
Native Language: . . . .
Religion – if converted, state also family religion: . . . .
Name of interviewer: . . . .
Place and date of interview: . . . .

1. When do you believe the unborn fetus has a soul?
2. At what stage of miscarriage would there be a burial ceremony?
3. Are there any things or events a pregnant woman is not to see?
4. Are there any jewelry or clothing a pregnant woman is not
   suppose to wear?
5. Are there any foods a pregnant woman should avoid? If so,
   which ones?
6. Can a pregnant woman communicate with her unborn child?
7. Does it make any sense for a father to rub the belly of his pregnant wife?
8. Does it make any sense for the mother to speak or sing to her
   unborn child?
9. Can an unborn child communicate his/her needs?
10. Can a baby learn before birth? If so, when does this capacity
    start?
11. Is divorce possible in your culture? If so, on what grounds?
    Who gets the children?
12. Do you know of any folktales relating to the sex of the child
    before birth?
13. What is the opinion about abortion in your culture? Is it legal?
    Is it undesirable?
14. What is the opinion about unwed motherhood in your cul-
    ture?
15. Please comment briefly on any customs with which you are
    familiar concerning the care of the unborn.

Questionnaire for Mothers

Name: . . . .
Country of origin and place of birth: . . . .
Date of birth: . . . .
Native language: . . . .
Religion – If converted, state family religion: . . . .
Number and ages of children: . . . .
Name of interviewer: . . . .
Place and date of interview: . . . .

1. When do you believe the unborn fetus has a soul?
2. If you were to miscarry, at what stage of the development of the unborn child would there be a burial ceremony? Would it be a religious ceremony or just a burial?
3. When you were pregnant, how did your husband treat you, i. e., were you told not to do heavy work or lift heavy objects?
4. Were any foods taboo?
5. Were there any things or events you were not supposed to see? If the rule was broken, what happened?
6. Was there any jewelry or clothing you should or should not wear?
7. Was there any point during pregnancy that sexual relations with your husband were taboo?
8. Was there any diet you should observe? Were there any foods you should avoid?
9. Did you sing, talk, or read to your unborn child?
10. Did you rub and massage your belly while pregnant to communicate with the child?
11. Was the newborn separated from you after birth? If so, at what age? Who cuts the umbilical cord? Do only women do it?
12. What is the attitude of your culture toward an unwed mother? Toward abortion?
13. Would you grieve more or less if you had an abortion vs. a miscarriage? (If you had an abortion, who induced you to have one? Were you forced to have one?)

Questionnaire for Mothers, continued

14. What is the father's role with the newborn? What is the grand-parents' role? What is the siblings' role with the newborn?
15. Can the unborn communicate his/her needs to the mother? What's your experience?
16. Can you increase a child's intelligence by reading and talking to him/her while still in the womb?
17. Could your unborn child learn?
18. If your sister were impregnated and not married, how would she be treated by the family?
19. Could you ever get a divorce in your culture? If so, on what grounds? Who initiates divorce proceedings? Who gets the children?
20. Did your family try to see that you had pleasant surroundings and that you were kept happy while pregnant?
21. If you craved certain foods, what happened?
22. Did the eating of certain foods increase the intelligence of your child?
23. Are there any folktales related to determining the sex of the children before birth? Can you tell the sex of the unborn and if so, how?
24. Was your husband present at your child's birth? Is this custo-mary? Is it desirable?
25. Do your other children have any role in prenatal care? Do they go to the hospital with the mother? Do they see the mother giving birth? Do they see the newborn right away?
26. Did your husband want your firstborn to be a son?
27. Do people choose a name before birth? Is this an informal decision or is there a naming ceremony before birth? Who chooses the name? What is the significance?
28. If one child were to die, is the next child to take the name of the dead child? Is this forbidden?
29. What happens in your culture if a woman is raped and im-pregnated? Does she have the child?

Questionnaire for Fathers

Name: . . . .

Country of origin and place of birth: . . . .

Date of birth: . . . .

Native language: . . . .

Religion – if converted, state family religion: . . . .

Are you a father? . . . .

Number and ages of children: . . . .

Are you a grandfather? . . . .

Name of interviewer: . . . .

Place and date of interview: . . . .

1. When do you believe the unborn fetus has a soul?
2. If a woman were to miscarry, at what stage of the development of the unborn child would there be a burial ceremony?
3. When she was pregnant how did you treat your wife?
4. Were any foods taboo?
5. Were there any things or events she was not supposed to see? If so, what happened?
6. Was there any jewelry or clothing she should or should not wear?
7. Was there any point in pregnancy that sexual relations between you and your wife were taboo?
8. Was there any diet or foods she should/shouldn't eat?
9. Did she sing, talk, or read to your unborn child? Did you do anything like this?
10. Did you rub and massage her belly while she was pregnant to communicate with the child?
11. Was the newborn separated after birth from the mother? If so, at what age? Who cuts the umbilical cord? Do only women do it?
12. What is the attitude of your culture toward an unwed mother? Toward abortion?
13. Would you grieve more or less if your wife had an abortion vs. a miscarriage? (Who induced? Was she forced to have an abortion?)

Questionnaire for Fathers, continued

14. What is the father's role with the newborn? What is the grand-parents' role? What is the siblings' role with the newborn?
15. Can the unborn communicate his/her needs to the mother? What's your opinion?
16. Can one increase a child's intelligence by reading and talking to it while it is a fetus?
17. Could an unborn child learn?
18. If your sister were impregnated and not married, how would she be treated by the family?
19. Could you ever get a divorce in your culture? If so, on what grounds? Who initiates divorce proceedings? Who gets the children?
20. Did your family try to see that your wife had pleasant surroundings and that she was kept happy while pregnant?
21. If she craved certain foods, what happened?
22. Did the mother's eating of certain foods increase the intelligence of your child?
23. Are there any folktales related to determining the sex of the children before birth? Can you tell the sex of the unborn and if so, how?
24. Were you present at your child's birth? Is this customary? Is it desirable?
25. Is there any role for other children in prenatal care? Do they go to the hospital with the mother? Do they see the mother giving birth?
26. Did you want your firstborn to be a son?
27. Do people choose a name before birth? Who chooses the name of the unborn? What is the significance?
28. If one child were to die, does the next child take the name of the dead child? Is this forbidden?

Questionnaire for Theologians

Name: . . . .
Country of origin and place of birth: . . . .
Native language: . . . .
Religion – if converted, state family religion: . . . .
Name of interviewer: . . . .
Date and place of interview: . . . .

1. According to your religion, at what time does the soul enter the body of a fetus? At conception? At what period of gestation? At birth? (In case of stillbirth, what determines the stage at which the soul enters the body?)
2. In case of miscarriage, is there a burial with/without religious ceremony? Is this related to the time of gestation when the miscarriage occurred?
3. What is the attitude toward abortion? If allowed, are there time limits or is allowance made for special cases?
4. What is the attitude toward rape? Of an unmarried woman? Of a married woman by her husband/by another man?
5. Does the husband have special obligations toward a wife during her pregnancy? What are these obligations?
6. Is there any point during pregnancy when sexual relations are discouraged or outright forbidden? At what time after delivery can sexual relations resume?
7. Are there any food restrictions for pregnant women?
8. Is there any jewelry or clothing that pregnant women should not wear?
9. What is the attitude toward an unwed mother?
10. Is divorce permitted in your religion? On what grounds? Who initiates the divorce proceedings? Who grants the divorce? Who gets the children?
11. Is it important where a child is conceived? Is the status of the father important for the time of conception or for birth?
12. What is the status of the first-born son?
13. Is the baby named before birth? Who chooses the name before/after birth? What is the significance? Distinguish choice of name and naming ceremony?

Questionnaire for Theologians, continued

14. If a child were to die/be stillborn/miscarried, can/should the
    next child take its name? Is this discouraged/forbidden?
15. Can the cradle be set up before birth?

Handout Chart

W. von Raffler-Engel, Institute for Public Policy Studies, Vanderbilt University, U.S.A.

8 weeks after conception	fully formed fetus
12 weeks after conception	brain waves can be registered
12 weeks after conception	skin is sensitive to touch
26 weeks after conception	can hear: heartbeat accelerates with louder noise, has jerking motions for sharp noises (like shooting)
26 weeks after conception	has taste: distinguishes sweet from sour substances (injected into amniotic fluid)
26 weeks after conception	can smell
35 weeks after conception	is sensitive to light (will turn towards source of light)

```
                        / inherited (instinctive)
                       /
Human behavior
                       \                  / in utero
                        \  learned      /
                          \ — after birth
```

Distributed during my lecture at the *Third International Conference on Cross-Cultural Communication: East and West*, Chen
Kung University, Taiwan, 1991.

The Life of the Unborn: Medical Evidence

Introduction

This book deals with the life of the fetus, as it is perceived by people in different cultures. By fetus, I mean the child developing in the uterus at any stage of pregnancy. The term fetus, in popular parlance, applies to the unborn in the mother's womb from the period of conception to birth. In precise terminology, the word fetus designates the intra-uterine offspring after eight weeks of gestation, when the embryo has developed recognizable human formations, such as the appendage of arms and legs.

The book only deals with the unborn who is growing in a woman's womb. I do not go into research of fertilization in vitro, nor do I study whether artificial insemination has any impact on maternal behavior during pregnancy. My sole concern is the mother and her child during gestation. As far as I know, I have restricted the interviews to women who had conceived through normal sexual intercourse.

In this chapter I want to show that there is absolutely no need to be skeptical when we hear that Japanese mothers play music when they are pregnant in order to foster musical aptitude in their child; or when an Indian mother tells us that she talks to her unborn to calm him/her. Western women do the same following a universal maternal instinct, but are slow to admit that they so do, or are not even consciously aware of what they are doing. Their denial is often less of a lie than lack of awareness.

Medical science is discovering more and more that the intra-uterine stage of human development is not restricted to the physical growth of the child. Gradually, the fetus acquires the use of the senses and it is correct to assume that he/she is capable of learning before birth (von Raffler-Engel 1988). I have supported this theory for many years. In this chapter I will provide stringent documentation to support this contention.

I do not go as far as some authors who consider birth only a minor event in the life of the child (Clauser 1971, p. 35). As much as I believe in communication before birth, the social life of the infant is much more varied than that of the fetus. I believe, however, that socialization initiates in utero and I see the fetus as a distinct human being. Fetal movement has been extensively studied and is amply reported in gynecological journals. There is no doubt in my mind that the fetus has its own little personality as "each fetus develops its own pattern of activity" (Rayburn 1987, p. 899).

Personalized fetal movement has been described as early as in the Bible where Rebekah's twins were said to be "struggling within her" (Genesis XXV, 22), as noted by the Danish physician Steen Neldam (1986, p. 213). Individual differences in the patterns of fetal movement were observed in a large scale study in Holland at the University Hospital of Groningen (de Vries et al. 1988).

The earliest physician who dealt with prenatal behavior was Hippocrates who lived in the fifth century B. C. E. He believed if suckling behavior were not already practiced in utero, babies could not be so efficient at it immediately after birth (Clauser 1971, p. 36). In the same vein, quite recently, an association has been documented "between prenatal behavior and infant behavior soon after birth" (Madison et al. 1986, p. 1479). The fetus also must be capable of feeling pain if "the premature infant responds to operative surgery, if analgesics are withheld, in the same way as adults (i. e., to painful stimuli)" (Dawes 1988, p. 543). That the fetus feels stress and pain during its birth is documented by the chemical reaction inside its brain which produces beta endorphin (Kiyoshi 1991).

Memory

The fetal brain also stores memories. Under hypnosis children will recount the events of their birthing (Kiyoshi 1991). It is by now common knowledge that babies who have been exposed to a consistent musical theme during their gestational period will calm down when this same theme is played after they are born. A most striking example is reported by Kiyoshi (1991). A friend of this author's teaches violin to children. One of his pupils, a three-year old girl, after learning how to play the violin, played a piece she had not been specifically taught. It was a piece to which her mother had listened every day while expecting this child.

Movement: The avoidance reaction

I will now present in chronological sequence the development of the sensory activities in the fetus as they are recorded in current bio-medical science. Of course, there are no absolutes and individual variations are present in the womb just as it is after birth. For a comprehensive treatment of fetal development I recommend the review article by Lyndon, Breckle and Wolfram (1983). A developmental chart is available on page 81 in an article by Mistretta and Bradley (1975).

When mothers say that they interpret the movements of the child they carry as a signal to them that their child is alive, they are quite correct. Indeed, their baby moves even before they can feel these movements. The first reaction of the fetus to a stimulus is avoidance. It moves away. As early as nine weeks after conception, "in response to a touch on the sole of his foot he will curl his toes or bend his hips and move away from the touching object" (Valman & Pearson 1980).

Brain waves

Bergstrom (1969) studied the EEG of fetuses immediately after separation from the maternal circulation and found rudimentary brain waves at 10 weeks of conceptual age; and at 17 weeks he was able to observe primitive wave patterns. Okamoto and Kirikae (1951) demonstrated slow brain activity with the use of cortical electrodes

Boyle County Public Library

at three months of conceptual age. But only at 32 to 35 weeks does the fetus begin to differentiate "between wakefulness, active sleep, and quiet sleep" (Niedermeyer and de Silva 1987, p. 135). After 36–38 weeks of gestation, premature babies "show EEG features that can be seen in full-term newborns" (Ibid, p. 136).

Sensitivity to touch

At eleven weeks that fetus can "produce complex facial expressions" (Valman & Pearson 1980) and at twelve weeks "he can close his fingers and thumb and he will open his mouth in response to pressure applied to the base of the thumb" (Ibid). Also, as early as ten and a half weeks of conceptual age the palms of the fetus' hands are sensitive to touch (Hill et al. 1983, p. 2388) and "by 15 to 17 weeks, sensitivity has spread to the abdomen and buttocks" (Ibid). The early development of sensitivity to touch may explain why women caress their abdomen as soon as they perceive they are pregnant.

Hearing

It is common that women sing when they are pregnant. In some cultures, like the Japanese, they do this with the avowed intent of being heard by the child in their womb. In the West, most women simply sing softly for the pleasure of a quiet moment to enjoy the thought of their impending motherhood. Many women, even in the Western world, which on the whole is insensitive to fetal manifestations, report that the baby in their womb moves rhythmically, or at least animatedly, when they sit in a concert hall or wherever loud music is played.

A series of research projects conducted in the late seventies and early eighties (Birnholz & Benacerall 1983, note 5) suggests that the human "auditory system is functional by the start of the third trimester" of pregnancy. These authors conducted their own research and observed a consistent blink response to noise in the fetus starting as early as 25 weeks of gestation. The absence of this startle effect was indicative of hearing deficits in the baby after birth. Subsequent research has further documented that "the cochlear function is indeed presently at the fifth month of gestation" (Sadovsky et al. 1986). The women reporting that their unborn children react to sound are correct. Maternal responses were tested at the Karolinska Institute at Danderyd Hospital in Sweden where the mother of healthy fetuses felt a kick immediately after the auditory stimulation (Westgren et al. 1987).

As the fetus matures, between 26 and 40 weeks of gestational age, his/her reaction to acoustic stimulation demonstrates "a functional maturation of the fetal central nervous system" (Gagnon et al. 1987, p. 1375). We all know that the perceptive and receptive power of the human being matures as he/she grows in the womb. What many people do not know is at what early period of gestation the baby's senses start being functional.

When a newborn is placed between two women who will speak at the same time and the baby can hear them but cannot see them, he/she will turn toward the mother (Brazelton and Tronik 1980). The newborn obviously recognizes the mother's voice. It is a voice familiar from the time before birth. I cannot prove that the fetus responds to his/her mother when she speaks or sings to her child in the womb, but I can prove that the mother is "the unborn's first significant other" (von Raffler-Engel 1988, p. 238).

Fetal response to external sounds has been amply researched. This is very important for the evaluation of maternal behavior toward the unborn. Not all researchers agree on the first period when a fetus reacts to an external auditory stimulus. The earliest seems to occur at 26 weeks of conceptual age (Wedenberg 1965). Women sing to their baby in the womb before that time. It is possible that further bio-medical research may reveal an earlier reaction. We see more and more that science lags behind common sense and old wives' tales. Maybe by the time this book gets into its second edition, I will have additional scientific information to match my naturalistic observations from around the world.

Taste

"Taste buds appear during the third month, and by the seventh month taste is probably established" (Monie 1983, p. 25). Mistretta and Bradley (1975, p. 80) summarize the research leading to this conclusion: "De Snoo (1937) reported that fetuses swallowed more amniotic fluid after an intra-amniotic injection of saccharin; Liley (1972) found that fetuses aged 34–39 weeks swallowed less after a noxious-tasting radio-opaque substance (Lipidiol) was injected into the amniotic fluid." That the fetus reacts to differences in taste does not imply that it monitors and selects the gustatory environment.

Olfaction

The sense of smell appears during the seventh month of conceptual age (Monie 1983, p. 25). It is generally believed that babies have a poor sense of smell, but this area may not have been adequately researched.

Sight

Fetuses are viable as early as five months of conceptual age, but only after seven months can they survive without extraordinary care. The eye develops very gradually in the fetus and only in approximately the seventh month, it becomes sensitive to light (Monie 1983, p. 24).

Voice

Although there are reports from physicians about fetuses crying in utero, modern day evidence acknowledges audible cries only during delivery when an adequate amount of air can enter the birth canal. During twin births, the second twin may be heard before it emerges after the first twin has been born (Parviainen 1949).

If you are an expectant mother, father or grandparent, or a sibling of the little life in the womb, I hope this rather dry, technical chapter has given you the certainty that you do not do something strange and irrational when you caress the maternal abdomen, sing or speak tenderly to the new life, as yet invisible, but already quite sensitive. You will then not be a stranger to the baby when it emerges to face the world.

For complete coverage of prenatal neurology. I would recommend the book edited by Prechtl (1984). An excellent summary is also available in the second chapter of the charming book about the newborn by Chamberlain (1988). Although I disagree with some of his conclusions, the book by Grobstein (1988) is also informative.

References

Bergstrom, R.M. (1969). Electrical parameters of the brain during ontogeny. In R.J. Robinson (Ed.), *Brain and early behavior* (pp. 15–37). London: Academic Press.

Birnholz, J.C. & Benacerraf, B.R. (1983). The development of human fetal hearing. *Science, 222* (4623) 516–518.

Brazelton, T.T. & Tronik, E. (1980). Preverbal communication between mothers and infants. In D,R. Olsen (Ed.), *The social foundation of language and thought. Essays in honor of J.S. Bruner* (pp. 299–315). New York: Norton.

Chamberlain, D. (1988). *Babies remember birth. And other extra-ordinary scientific discoveries about the mind and personality of your newborn.* New York: Ballantine Books.

Clauser, G. (1971). *Die vorgeburtliche Entstehung der Sprache als anthropologisches Problem: Der Rhythmus als Organisator der menschlichen Entwicklung.* Stuttgart: Ferdinand Enke Verlag.

Dawes, G.S. (1988). The development of fetal behavioral patterns (The 1987 James A. F. Stevenson Memorial Lecture). *Canadian Journal of Physiology and Pharmacology, 66,* 541–548.

de Snoo, K. (1937). Das trinkende Kind in Uterus. *Monatschrift für Geburtshilfe und Gynäkologie, 105,* 88–97.

de Vries, J.I.P., Visser, G.H.A. & Prechtl, H.F.R. (1988). The emergence of fetal behavior. III. Individual differences and consistencies. *Early Human Development, 16,* 85–103.

Gagnon, R., Hunse, C., Carmichael, L., Fellows, F. & Patrick, J. (1987). Human fetal responses to vibratory acoustic stimulation from twenty-six weeks to term. *American Journal of Obstetrics and Gynecology, 157,* 1375–1381.

Grobstein, C. (1988). *Science and the unborn: Choosing human futures.* New York: Basic Books.

Hill, L.M., Breckle, R. & Wolfram, K.R. (1983). An ultrasonic view the developing fetus. *Obstetrical and Gynecological Survey, 38,*375–398.

Kiyoshi, Oshima 1991. Memory of the fetus *Gendaishiso* (October), p. 72–86.

Liley, A.W. (1972). Disorders of amniotic fluid P. In N.S. Assali & C.R. Brinkman III (Eds.), *Pathophysiology of gestation, Vol. III: Fetal-placental disorders* (pp. 157–206). New York & London: Academic Press.

Madison, L.S., Madison, J.K. & Adubato, S. (1986). Infant behavior and development in relation to fetal movement and habituation. *Child Development, 57,* 1475–1482.

Mistretta, C.M. & Bradley, R.M. (1975). Taste and swallowing in utero: A discussion of fetal sensory function. *British Medical Bulletin, 31,* p. 80–84.

Monie, I.W. (1983). Development and physiology of the fetus. Chapter 5 in Albert B. Gerbie & John J. Sciarra (Eds.), *Gynecology and obstetrics, Vol. 2* (rev. ed.). Philadelphia: Harper & Row.

Niedermeyer, E. & Lopez da Silva, F. (1987). *Electroencephalography. Basic principles, clinical applications and related fields* (2nd ed.). Baltimore-Munich: Urban & Schwarzenberg.

Neldam, S. (1986). Fetal movement as an indicator of fetal well being. *Danish Medical Bulletin, 33,* 213–221.

Okamoto, Y. & Kirikae, T. (1951). EEG studies on brain of fetus of children of premature birth. *Folia Psychiatricae Neurologica Japanica, 5,* 135–146.

Parviainen, S. (1949). Vagitus uterinus. *Annales Chirugiae et Gynecologiae Fenniae, 38,* 330–336.

Prechtl, H.F.R. (1984). Continuity of neural functions from prenatal to postnatal live. *Clinics in Developmental Medicine, 94.* Oxford: Spastics International Medical Publications, Blackwell Scientific Publications Ltd./Philadelphia: J.B. Lippincott Co.

Rayburn, W.E. (1987). Monitoring fetal body movement. *Clinical Obstetrics and Gynecology, 3,* 889–911.

Sadovsky, E., Samueloff, A., Sadovsky, Y., Ohel, G. (1986). Incidence of spontaneous and evoked fetal movements. *Gynecolic and Obstetric Investigation, 21,* 177–181.

Valman, H.B. & Pearson, J.F. (1980). What the fetus feels. *British Medical Journal, 280* (6209), 233–234.

von Raffler-Engel, W. (1988). The synchronous development of language and kinesics: Further evidence. In M.E. Landsberg (Ed.), *The genesis of language: A different judgment of evidence* (pp. 227–246) (Selected papers from the Symposium on Language Origins, XIth International Congress of Anthropological and Ethnological Sciences, University of British Columbia, 1983) Berlin: Mouton de Gruyter).

Wedenberg, E. (1965). Prenatal tests of hearing. *Acta Otolaryngologica* (Supplement) *206,* 27.

Westgren, M., Alstrom, H., Nyman, M. & Ulmsten, U. (1987). Maternal perception of sound-provoked fetal movements as a measure of fetal well-being. *British Journal of Obstetrics and Gynecology, 94,* 523–527.

Folk Beliefs About the Unborn Child from Around the World

Introduction

When I talked about my perception of pregnancy and the relationship of the mother with her unborn child, many people told me that they don't really believe that the unborn can communicate, but that there are many superstitions on that subject. Some of my respondents insisted that the lower classes are superstitious while they themselves are not. Others mentioned that their elders cling to superstitions which they have surpassed.

I collected a fair amount of "superstitions," but I find it no easy task to present them to the readers. Let's begin with "religious superstitions." These, of course, are in the eyes of the beholder. For the freethinker, all reported "facts" that cannot be scientifically documented are superstitious. For the religious, such facts are true when recognized by his religion, and superstition when they fall within another belief system.

Somewhere in between religious tenets and superstitions are folk traditions. People will say that they really don't believe that a certain practice has any validity and that it really amounts to pure superstition, but that they observe it nevertheless out of "respect for tradition." The same is often true for religious usages.

Allowing for the above classification, there seems to be no superstition that is classified as such by everybody. How then does one define superstition in absolute terms? Anthropologists define superstition as "a belief for which there is no real basis in either science or religion" (Winick 1977, p. 516). I have already mentioned religion and showed that its relation to superstition is more complex than this.

The complexity of this relationship was already recognized by the ancient Greeks. Plutarch (1970) after advising that "If you perform and observe constantly the accepted rites ... you will avoid superstition, which is no less an evil than atheism" (II. p. 135), comments that "Some, erring completely, have slipped into superstition, and others, shunning it like marsh, have unwittingly fallen in turn over the precipice of atheism" (67, p. 225).

Psychologists dislike the term "superstition" for its vagueness. For them "Beliefs having no reference to the magical or supernatural, even though scientifically insupportable, are better called disbeliefs ... The assertion of a natural cause-effect relation between a maternal fright and a birthmark is better described as unscientific" (English & English 1970, p. 536).

The latter example is particularly apt to bring us to think about what is scientific. In absolute terms, it is the opposite of superstitious. Real facts can be documented scientifically. That is, they can be proven correct through standardized testing and their occurrence can be predicted, given identical circumstances. There is only one hitch to scientificity. Testing procedures and technical equipment improve over time and some of what was classified as superstitious becomes factual. It is also possible that errors in research will be uncovered and what was classified as proven gets rejected into the realm of superstition. When reading the chapter on the medical evidence of the activity of the fetus, much that was believed mere "old wives' tales" not too long ago will appear to be possible without doubt. Whether the presumed relationship between a pregnant woman's fright and her baby's birthmark is superstitious or may one day be scientifically documented, remains to be seen. One cannot exclude such possibility.

The word "scientific" is a bit restrictive nowadays. The documentary value of a vast amount of empirical evidence to my mind is a form of factual proof. Nobody questions that the normal period for gestation is nine months and no scientific laboratory test is required to prove this.

In the following pages I will present the results of my inquiry about superstitions among diverse groups of people. I use the heading superstition because it is an easily recognizable wording for usages and beliefs that cannot be scientifically justified. But I wish to make clear that I do not posit any value judgments either about the absurdity or about the validity of the usages and beliefs that have come to my attention.

What I want to bring to the attention of the readers is that, as in old folktales, we must consider an unborn child's general environment outside the maternal womb. Medical science has vindicated the belief that the fetus has an autonomous existence and is directly susceptible to environmental influences rather than exclusively through the intermediary of its mother. When a baby remembers the music it has heard before its birth, we can no longer doubt that there is a direct interaction between the fetus and the outside world. We now know from medical tests that the fetus possesses intelligence and memory. To ignore this is as unrealistic as to take all old folktales at face value.

I do not deny that some of the usages I came across seemed awfully strange to me and some I found plainly absurd; but I do not discount the impact of autosuggestion and some usages may have the same beneficial effects as placebo pills. It is in this spirit that I want the readers to share the information I gathered from personal interviews as well as from the literature. From the research I have conducted, I have come to see the child in the womb as an individual human being, incompletely formed as it may be.

This is how the unborn is perceived in most Asian, Middle Eastern (including the Bible), African and Native American cultures. This is how it was originally perceived in the West, until, at a certain period in the history of Western philosophical and medical thinking, the child in the womb started being considered only as a passive entity. In ancient Greece, medical texts described the fetus very much like a living child. The father of Western medicine, Hippocrates, in his treatise on "The nature of the child," says when the nutrients from the placenta "are no longer sufficient and the child is already big, in its desire for more nutriment than is there, it tosses about and so ruptures the membranes" (Lloyd

1978, p. 343). It took two millennia to gain the medical knowledge to confirm the Greek doctor (see McDonald and Nathanielsz in the introductory chapter). The fetus does indeed have an active part in the timing of its birth. It is not just "expelled" through the contractions of its mother or "extracted" with the help of the obstetrician.

Cultures and religions differ in the treatment of a miscarried fetus. The subject of burial rites for the unborn will be the topic of a separate chapter. Here I only want to bring out that the responses of the people I interviewed clearly suggest that the late nineteen hundreds signal a return to the acceptance of the unborn as a member of the group. Until recently, particularly among the most advanced nations, only folk beliefs preserved the original concept of an intelligent, active fetus while science and education fostered a different approach. We have now reached a turning point where medical research is advanced enough to re-evaluate the beliefs of our forebears.

Until a generation ago, in the affluent nations of the Western world, the human fetus was looked upon as a passive entity. To grow properly all "it" (never "he" or "she") needed was an adequate food supply from the placenta. The only recognition of outside influence was a warning to the mother to keep out of stress because that would disturb the hormonal balance and this could affect the fetus. It was all physical and confined to the inside of the mother's body. Only folk beliefs among the "uneducated" preserved the old, original concept of an intelligent, active child-to-be.

Today, among the "educated," more and more parents wonder whether they can do something to increase their unborn child's intelligence. Not all believe they can, but most try anyway, just in case. That the newborn recognizes in the outside world what was familiar to it (or should I say, him/her?) from before birth is now a medically proven fact. Whether the intelligence of the unborn can be improved is not proven with certainty, but as I will show from the tales of old, such belief is among the most ancient.

Modern up-to-date medical research has validated the ancient concept and given credence to the gist of old wives' tales. Myths and superstitions are not meant to be taken literally. They are intended to illustrate a profound truth which underlies some fantastic story. When they talk about life before birth, these folktales are embellishments, an elaboration on the very real communicative abilities of the unborn. The maternal instinct is correct when it leads a woman to sing to the child she carries and to caress the area of her body where she feels the child moving, just as later on she will sing lullabies and cuddle her infant. Birth is not as abrupt a passage as was generally believed in the modern world.

Cultures in older times and surviving folk traditions also consider the general environment outside the womb. For them the fetus has a much more autonomous existence and is directly susceptible to environmental influences rather than exclusively through the intermediary of his mother. Recent medical findings have vindicated the older beliefs in the direct interaction between the fetus and the outside world. Folktales about unborn children overhearing conversations and talking from the womb are grounded on the very real capability of the fetus to interact with the outside environment. It is, of course, not possible that an unborn child can converse in real language, but to ignore the capability of the fetus to sense and to respond to events outside his mother is equally unrealistic.

Recent bio-medical research has documented beyond doubt that there is an association between prenatal behavior and the behavior of the newborn. The fetus also must be capable of pain if an infant born prematurely shows expression of pain during surgery. Sad to say, it is only quite recently that pain killers are being administered to the newborn just as they are to older children in case of an operation. I shudder to think how much pain these little creatures have endured in the past. But, then, until not too long ago, even young infants were operated on without anesthesia, all in the erroneous belief that being so far from adulthood, they were not yet capable of experiencing pain like a fully developed organism does.

Medical science is discovering more and more that as the fetus grows in size and its organs develop, its senses mature just as well, much earlier than previously believed. I have over the past thirty years observed the sensory development of the newborn and am convinced that already in the womb the child can receive information and communicate its desires.

The very earliest sensory perceptions of the fetus are circumscribed by the uterus. Later, as more of its senses develop, it perceives some of what goes on beyond the watery sac and its mother's body. The first reaction to an external stimulus is avoidance; it moves away. As early as nine weeks after conception, a fetus will respond to a touch on the sole of its foot by curling its toes or bending its hips and moving away from the touching object. Is this only an automatic reflex like when we retract our hand when it strikes a burning stove? As severely retarded people do not necessarily react that way, we must assume a modicum of intelligence in the fetus.

The avoidance reaction of the unborn represents an early stage, if not the earliest of the cognitive development of the child. It may sound strange to many people to assume reasoning as early as two months after conception. As the Latin proverb says, "natura non facet saltum," nothing in nature happens all of a sudden. If reasoning were not present in some rudimentary form in the fetus, it would be hard to explain how it appears later. In the physical as well as the intellectual realm everything develops by gradual steps until it reaches maturity. The maturation of the intellect begins at conception, parallel to the maturation of the body.

Babies communicating from the womb

The saga of mother-child interaction before birth is universal. The Chinese empress Tai-zan who lived in the 13th century B.C. "commenced the instruction of her child when he was still in her womb" (Stucken 1907, p. 199). In the Finnish creation myth, Wainamoinen complained that life in the womb was too confining, dark and narrow, and begged to get out (Kalevala I, 289–308; in Stucken 1907, p. 199). In the Indian legend of Ashtavakra, a child recites the Vedas while still in the womb. In another Indian saga, a child in the womb holds back the semen of a man who forced himself on his mother (Stucken 1907, p. 201).

A computer search of the literature revealed an incredible amount of reports about babies crying, and even speaking, while they were in the womb. I was thus a bit surprised that I found no such mention by the people I interviewed nor on the replies to my questionnaires. Crying is not completely impossible. Articulated speech, however, is. Even if they are equipped with a couple of teeth, as happens occasionally, that babies can speak before birth is impossible from scientific as well as empirical evidence.

The earliest possible occurrence of a consistent word-like expression is at the age of three months (von Raffler-Engel 1964). Rare occurrences of regular words may be found at five months, but normally not before nine months. Occurrences of prenatal speech reported in the literature were indeed termed miraculous in those folktales. The definition of a miracle implies that an event has passed the boundary between what is naturally possible and what goes beyond.

From my point of view, the interesting aspect of such reports is that, at a certain stage of development, it is hard to draw the line between crying and rudimentary forms of speaking (von Raffler-Engel 1964), and that it is physically possible to hear a baby cry before it is fully delivered (see medical chapter). It is thus proven that babies can cry while inside the womb, but they can be heard only when an adequate amount of air can enter the birth canal. Without this volume of air the fetal cries would be too faint to be audible. During a twin birth, the second twin may be heard after the first twin has been born. Chamberlain (1988, p. 69) has been told that "if there were air in the womb, the fetus could be heard crying much of the time."

From the ample literature about babies crying in the womb, I have selected a cross section from all over the world in various periods of history. Many of these legends talk of twins quarrelling over who will be born first. This is a universal motif because so many societies attach legal importance to the right of the firstborn. Some twins are reported as talking, others limit their quarrels to physical clashes. The latter are quite possible but not for a legalistic cause.

The Bible mentions that the twins Esau and Jacob "struggled together" in their mother's womb (Genesis XXV, 22). They already represented "two nations" (Genesis XXV, 22). At their birth Jacob held his hand on "his brother's heel" (Genesis XXV, 26) as if to pull him back and prevent him from being the firstborn (Hosea XII, 4).

In Greek mythology, Zeus is believed to have had a twin brother. The name of his twin varies, but it is always mentioned that he fought with him in the womb (Krappe 1973, p. 31). Similarly, in Greek antiquity, Apollodorus (1954, p. 145) tells of

Abas' twin sons, Acrisius and Proteus, who "quarrelled with each other while they were still in the womb, and when they grew up, they waged war for the kingdom." Like the Biblical twins, they clashed over territory, implying that the unborn has consciousness and makes willful decisions.

Even though a fight for subsequent national dominance is evidently an attribution post factum, territorial fights inside the womb are factually correct. The stronger twin will gather wider territory for moving its limbs and gain better access to the food supply. In twin births often the first to come out is larger and heavier than its weaker sibling.

A century later, the widely traveled Greek writer Plutarch (1970, 12, p. 137; in Kahlo 1930/1933, p. 520) recounts that in Egypt the divine twins Isis and Osiris started their sexual relationship "in the darkness of the womb." The fruit of their union was Aroueris, "who is called Horus by the Egyptians and Apollos by the Greeks." What interests me in this myth is that the loving relationship between the Egyptian twins started before they were born and continued throughout their lives. Birth is not a momentous event either for their own relationship or for the continuation of their lineage.

Among North American Indians too, I found legends about twins quarrelling in the womb. The Iroquois tell of a woman impregnated by the West Wind, (Thompson 1929, p. 277, Note 21; in Thompson 1946, p. 307) and whose twins quarrelled about who will be born first (Thompson 1929, p. 279–280, Note 33; in Thompson 1946, p. 307).

Twins have exerted fascination throughout the ages, but not all quarrel with each other. In an Angolan legend (Chatelain 1894, p. 85), a woman ready to give birth to twins, first hears the elder child talking from her belly. After he is delivered, the younger child speaks from the womb before he is born. They both keep right on talking when they are out of their mother's belly. Both continue to be helpful to their parents, just as each of them kindly advised their mother before she was to give birth to them: "Mother, place thyself well now, I am coming here."

The Angolan twins are in the minority as they talk to their mother rather than communicate with each other. They fall into a category of children who from the womb speak to their mother in order to assist her or speak out in her defense, or, in rare instances, speak out against her in defense of somebody else.

Babies symbolize innocence and it seems that such symbolism is apparent even before birth. In a South American Indian myth, an unborn child guides his mother to find her husband/his father. This child so actively communicates with his mother that he grows angry and remains silent when he is refused a request (Metraux 1948, p. 132). One other popular South American Indian unborn god-child assists his mother, Coatlicue, who was frightened when her older sons marched against her to kill her. But one of their army communicated with her unborn child, who, in turn, commanded his mother to have no fear (Alexander 1920, p. 60).

One child, however, turns against his mother for the sake of justice. In a Moorish folktale, a child talks from the womb accusing his mother of murder in order to save an innocent man of being wrongly accused (Rivière & Starkweather 1901, in Bolte & Polívka 1963, p. 535).

Kahlo (1930/1933, p. 520) lists authors who tell of "legendary heroes who hold conversations while in the womb." Heller (1930/1933, p. 102) reports that Islamic tradition makes frequent mention of children who speak either while still in the womb or soon after birth. He cites the legends of Abraham, Joseph, Jesus, and St. George. In Iranian mythology it is said of the very wise Aoshnara that "While yet in his mother's womb, he taught many a marvel and at his birth he was able to confound Angra and Mainyu by answering all the questions and riddles of Fracih, the unbeliever" (Carnoy 1917, p. 335).

The conception of Zarathustra was divine. "His guardian angel entered into an haoma plant, and passed with its juice into the body of a priest as the latter offered divine sacrifice; at the same time a ray of heaven's glory entered the bosom of the maid of noble lineage" (Durant 1935, p. 364). Like most mythical figures, he was very mature at birth. He is said to have laughed aloud "on the very day of his birth" which made the evil spirits flee (Ibid). We are reminded of medieval paintings of the Madonna with child were the baby Jesus is generally disproportionately large.

In the Christian New Testament, we read that after the annunciation, Mary the Mother of Jesus arose and went to her cousin Elizabeth's house. Elizabeth was old and had been barren, but now was with child. She was carrying the person to be known as John the Baptist. When Mary greeted her cousin, "It came to pass, that, when Elizabeth heard the salutation of Mary, the babe leaped in her womb; and Elizabeth was filled with the Holy Ghost: and she spake with a loud voice and said, 'Blessed are thou among women, and blessed is the fruit of thy womb!' " Elizabeth proclaims to her cousin that her unborn child leapt with joy in her womb as soon as he heard her greeting (Luke 1:41–42).

African heroes manifest their special status before they are born. Two Angolan heroes speak while still in the womb and one of them eats a whole ox immediately after he is born (Werner 1925, p. 2131). Among the Zulu, a woman hears her unborn child admonishing her to give birth to him. The woman tells her husband that she has a prodigy who can speak before he is born, but the child says nothing because he speaks only when he is alone with his mother. After his birth he cuts his umbilical cord by himself. A Christian writer, the Rev. Callaway (1868, p. 6), after telling about this, makes the caustic comment that the Zulu folktale was meant to produce laughter, whereas asserting that "St. Benedict sang eucharistic hymns in his mother's womb" is a "pious fraud and thus far less innocuous."

With the advent of Christianity, we find saints instead of heroes. Children who speak prematurely "form a large quota of miracles" (Loomis 1948, p. 23). One such child "made peace between the king and his father by speaking from his mother's womb" (Plummer 1910, vol. I, p. 66; in Loomis 1948, p. 23). Another child "spoke three times from his mother's body before he was born" (Acta Sanctorum Oct, VI, 302, col. 1; in Loomis 1948, p. 23). Tuan MacCairill, of Celtic mythology, was a good listener. He overheard many conversations while in the womb and became a prophet when he grew up. He was a forerunner of Christianity and he was baptized in St. Patrick's time (Macculloch 1918, p. 207).

These children, aptly called "Wonder Children" by one collector of such tales (Loomis 1948), have a consciousness of their own. They make decisions and have fights. Their mother is not the medium through which they receive outside stimuli. She is only the place where they are housed and fed. They are taken care of in a manner not radically dissimilar to the position they hold after birth.

One is reminded of the legal quibbles of Europe during the Middle Ages. Courtiers and clerics of that time discussed whether the status of the emperor's son conceived "in the purple," that is when his father had already ascended the throne, was higher than that of the son born first to him in natural order but conceived before he had become emperor.

Nowadays such a debate seems really strange to us. What Western law has been involved with in recent times is the status of a man's children born out of wedlock. These children, formerly ignored, now have inheritance rights and may adopt their father's surname. The most famous case is that of Elvis Presley, Jr. In American family law the firstborn has no special rights, but the title could be claimed only by the child born first within a legal marriage whereas now it goes to any child that can reasonably claim to be the one born first.

Community acceptance of the child

In the Western society, the woman's womb is not considered part of the world, only a female organ. But this may change, considering the ongoing legal battle on whether frozen embryos can be equated with living children. Our perspective on when the product of human conception is to be awarded the respect we owe to a person may change radically over the next years. For the time being, in Western society, a child is considered part of the community after it enters the world where everybody else lives.

In some Third World societies, the child is welcome as soon as a pregnancy is discovered. "From the beginning, right after conception, we know it is a person," said a black woman from Liberia. She also said that the family has great expectations for the child and arrangements may be made for marriage at an early stage of pregnancy, provided the child turns out to be a girl.

This custom is not too dissimilar from that of affluent parents in America that enroll their children in prestigious schools before they are born to make sure they will be admitted later on. Now we also have people living in communes where everybody shares the joy of expecting parents. In Liberia bearing a child is an honor and in the rural areas abortion is virtually non-existent. No expenses are spared to pamper the pregnant woman and the whole village rubs her tummy. They tell stories and talk to the unborn child because it is already considered part of the group.

Marital relations

There are many superstitions associated with the taboo of sexual relations of a man with his pregnant wife. The Laotians believe that if he as much as sleeps in the same room with her, he will "disturb the soul of the fetus."

In polygamous societies, abstinence from a pregnant wife is no hardship. Where monogamy is the rule, it is seldom demanded. Unfaithfulness is, however, more harshly condemned when the wife is pregnant.

In Zaire, when an unfaithful husband returns to his pregnant wife, he endangers the fetus and may poison it. As punishment, after she delivers, he must sit at the foot of her bed and confess by naming the other woman. For his punishment, his wife's parents will take her and the newborn home with them for several months. In order to get his wife back, he must go to her parents together with his own parents and ask forgiveness for having posed a danger to the child.

The protection of the expected child is always the prime concern. A woman from Lima, Peru, said that if it became known that a man was unfaithful during his wife's pregnancy, nobody should tell her about it because the trauma it would cause her would harm her as well as the unborn.

The care of the expectant mother

Most societies pay attention to the expectant mother even though not all do so for a woman who is pregnant outside matrimony. In Europe, until not too long ago, such women were not considered worthy of care because the expected child was none but "the wages of sin."

But now, regardless of the status of the child, in most cultures, as soon as it becomes apparent that a child is expected, people will accord kindly treatment to the mother because they believe that any discomfort caused her would harm the child she carries. It is said that an unhappy mother will bear an unhappy child. This is a very interesting observation because it shows that folk wisdom realizes that the fetus does not develop only physically, but also mentally even though the average person never thinks of any development beyond the physical growth and well-being.

The widespread belief that a strong emotion felt by the mother may produce a birthmark in her offspring does not interest me to the same degree as do reports on the direct communication of the fetus with his mother. Unless the impact of maternal emotions implies empathy on the part of the child, the transmission is purely physiological. In all cultures there are numerous reports of birthmarks of strawberries or other edibles resulting from a woman's craving for food that could not be satisfied. Even in societies where women have very low status, their craving for special foods when they are pregnant is supposed to be satisfied at any cost. All fathers who compiled my questionnaires replied that when their pregnant wife wanted a certain food, "she got it." They even cite some instances where procuring the particular edible was extremely cumbersome for them, including a three-hour drive both ways.

There are numerous tales of pregnant women being frightened by an animal, a fire, or other fearful occurrence, which will leave a birthmark on the fetus. The injunction to "keep a pregnant woman happy" is universal. Cultures vary in what expectant mothers should, or must, avoid.

Avoidance of funerals

Most widespread is the prohibition to attend funerals. Among other countries, it is ascertained by Ruud (1980, p. 243) for Madagascar. Among the people interviewed for this book, it was reported by a native of Nigeria as well as one of Zaire. In other cultures it is not an injunction, but a custom, essentially a good advice for a pregnant woman.

This is the case for Jewish women expecting a child. In general, they do not go to the cemetery, but a rabbi would not discourage a woman from going to her father's funeral if this is what she felt comfortable doing. The main point is that she should be as little upset as possible.

The same principle underlies the Japanese custom where a pregnant woman is discouraged, but not prohibited from attending a funeral.

In China, pregnant women are not supposed to see a dead person because the dead person may carry away the child, (Yu Xuegong, personal information). Considering that the Chinese honor their dead by exposing him or her in their homes for a week before burial, it makes a lot of sense for a pregnant woman to avoid contact with the corpse.

Hindus also admonish pregnant women not to see the dead and they are not allowed to go to a funeral, my son was told by a physician from Bombay.

Christian white Americans attend funerals, but some Black Americans believe that if they do, the child in the womb will come to look like the dead person.

Many more societies do not allow, or discourage, pregnant women from attending funerals. The underlying reason, as in most folk customs, is a sensible one. A woman with child should be happy and not be in the company of sad people. To make sure such sensible injunctions are obeyed, they are couched in forbidding terms. A good example is when in China it is said that a dead person may snatch the unborn child, as I reported above.

Envious spirits

In many parts of the world the fetus will be protected against envious spirits. The most common amulet is the evil eye, an image of a human eye. In South America, such amulet is made of ceramic and worn around the neck or pinned to the woman's clothes. In Sicily, the evil eye is called "il fascinatore," the enchanter, and still commonly used today. Belief in the malevolent power of some people's eyes, their "evil eye," is still widespread and common, and I feel sorry for these persons.

Another common amulet is the horseshoe. Horseshoes are used as good luck charms for general purposes in may parts of the world. In Guatemala, during an eclipse or a storm, a pregnant woman must wear a horseshoe amulet or her baby will be deformed.

In the mountains of Northern Italy, women in advanced stages of pregnancy stay home with windows tightly closed. They could have a sudden delivery and until the baby was baptized, the devil could take possession of its soul if he only found a way to enter the room where the child came into the world. After the child is born, when it is carried to the church to be baptized it is tightly covered and carefully watched. I know of one case, some fifty years ago, where the baby was so solidly covered that it suffocated. The parents had it baptized immediately in the hope they were still in time to save its soul.

The expectation of a child is a joyous event and the woman has to be guarded against envy. Anticipation is therefore discouraged. Muslims in some countries make preparations only after the sixth month of gestation. In Madagascar and in some parts of Turkey mothers and relatives do not sew baby clothes until the child is safely born. Religious Jews do not ready the room for the new baby until after the child is born and sure to survive. All these customs date from times when stillbirths and infant deaths were common and protected the parents from severe disappointments.

Pablo Picasso did not care to take his pregnant mistress to see a doctor because "he shared the primitive belief that to exhibit too much concern about a pregnancy is to invite disaster" (Sorel 1948, p. 30).

Among Guatemalans of Spanish descent, pregnant women wear a little bag filled with garlic and special herbs on a necklace or as a bracelet to ward off bad spirits. If a woman is not protected in this fashion, the baby inside her may explode. After the baby is born, it is given a little bag filled with red seeds to wear for protection. Red is the color strong enough to ward off bad spirits. In a similar vein, Native Americans are said to have "strong blood" and are feared by pregnant women and mothers of infants in the population of Spanish origin.

Native Americans themselves smoke cigars to keep away bad spirits that someone might have given to the baby before or after birth. White women often consult a witch when they are pregnant and are often advised to use the smoke from a cigar to dispel an evil spirit. All this was told to my son by a couple from Guatemala who were of Spanish descent and who had three children, but never did any of these things and were very well disposed toward the Native Americans. They explained that many people observe these practices without really believing in their efficacy, but still wanted to play it safe.

In Brazil, in addition to carrying garlic in her pocket, a pregnant woman during the entire period of her gestation will get a small bell and carry it between her breasts. The purpose is always to ward off envious spirits that could harm the baby. I do not know of any other place where a bell is used for this purpose, but garlic is very common.

In the Bavarian and Austrian Alps, fifty years ago, garlic was used to protect small children from disease as well as from evil spirits; and this usage, albeit less common, is still practiced today. In Nicaragua special herbs are added to the garlic to protect the pregnant woman, and the same is attached to the clothing of the baby once it is born. Garlic is also put at the doorsteps to the delivery room and the baby's room so that evil spirits cannot enter. There is hardly any family in South America interviewed by my son who does not mention garlic as a potent defense against envious spirits.

The idea that the baby will suffer if its mother elicits ill feelings from somebody is widespread. Black Americans believe that if a pregnant woman pokes fun at somebody, the baby will come to look like that person.

Benign spirits

All over the world, the fear of evil spirits seems to be stronger than the confidence in benign spirits. There seem to be so many more practices to deflect negative influences than practices to invoke positive spirits. Many prayers to the good spirits are asking for their help to ward off the bad ones.

In Laos, the expectant mother may wear any jewelry she wishes. But after she gives birth, during the first two months, she should not wear any jewels. Following the precepts of the Buddha, she must not exhibit greed or materialism so that good spirits will surround her baby. One woman added that this was a very private time where one does not show off.

Birthmarks

I now will recount the many things pregnant women should do or not do, look at or avoid seeing. About as universal as the barring of a woman with child from attending to the dead which I have reported earlier, is the belief that certain actions will lead to the formation of a birthmark or other reminder on the baby's body.

Ms. Sue Reynolds, one of the many kindly people who helped in gathering data for this book, went to the Appalachian hills of Tennessee, an area known for its isolation from much of the rest of the state. She questioned an eighty-five-year-old woman who was said to be well versed in the folklore of her people. Most of her fellow villagers share her belief that if, during the first trimester of pregnancy, the expectant mother has a scary impression, that impression will leave its mark on the child. But for some of the younger generation, she does seem a bit extreme and when she started telling her story, one young man left the room because such storytelling was "the time when the witches fly."

The good woman recounted that "When Durwood was born he had a red, bloody spot on his leg, because a horse had his leg hurt and was bleeding and his mother knowed (sic) it wouldn't do to touch her face, so she touched her leg." When she was pregnant herself, she was scared of a snake, and when her baby girl was born, "she wiggled from side to side." When she was expecting her second child, she was asked by her husband to go into a hog pen and drive a hog out. The sow bit her on the leg and the baby girl was club-footed.

Fife (1976) has collected a great amount of folklore among the Mormons on the transmission of an unpleasant maternal impression to the unborn child in the form of a birthmark which "resembles the object or circumstance which produced the mother's emotional state" (Fife 1976, p. 274).

According to a woman from Afghanistan interviewed for this book, in her country it is believed that if a pregnant woman sees the full moon, her baby will have a birthmark on the face or the eye. Given that the cycle of the moon phases parallels the cycle of the menstrual flow, it is understandable that the moon plays a large part in the lore of pregnancy. In Venezuela, a cousin of mine tells me, walking at night under the full moon produces birthmarks.

Turkish Muslims as well as Jews believe that if a pregnant woman is touched, the baby will have a birthmark on the correspond-
ing part of its body. If an object falls on her, the baby will have a
birthmark looking like that object. It is recommended to eat
strawberries with care lest one is accidentally dropped while eating. Strawberries, by the way, seem to be among the most frequently cited sources of birthmarks; probably because the shape
of many birthmarks can easily be described as looking in color
and design like one such berry.

Women will also have to be very careful with what they touch.
If they touch a liver spot, the baby in Turkey, will have such spots.
They also must be careful with what they eat. In Turkey, if the
mother-to-be eats quinces, the baby will have dimples. Of course,
it is impossible to cover the entire world. That I can tell so much
about Turkey is simply the result of my son, who did the bulk of
the interviewing, happening to have many Turkish friends.

In Afghanistan, a pregnant woman must not go outside during
an eclipse of the sun. She must be careful to hide from the eclipse.
If she looks at the sun, a middle-class woman from that country
told my then researcher Ms. S. Reynolds, her child will be born
with a burn mark on the face.

Birthmarks can also be the result of some wrongdoing on the
part of the mother-to-be. If this sounds very moralistic, one is still
confounded with the question of why the little baby will be dis-
figured because of its mother's reprehensible deed. I assume that
most cultures identify with the type of generational transmission
of good and evil so sternly expressed in the Hebrew Bible, and
underlying the Oriental ancestor cults.

In the vein of morality rather than accident, the Muslims in
Turkey attribute less importance to scares from the outside than
to the uneasy feeling that comes from not doing the right thing.
If a pregnant woman takes something without the permission of
the owner, her child will bear the mark of this object. One Turkish
woman told my son that she has no birthmarks because her
mother never took any food without the permission of her mother.
When women just take a simple piece of fruit without its owner's
permission, their child will have such a birthmark.

It can even get more complicated, if a pregnant woman takes a
pomegranate without the permission of its owner and makes holes
in it so that she can suck it, her child will never be able to have a

bucket that does not have a hole. In the rural areas of Turkey this is still commonly believed.

As widespread as stories about birthmarks are, the only underlying reality seems to be that expectant mothers need to be sheltered from frightening events and satisfied to the point that is possible when they have cravings for food. All physicians I talked to believe that birthmarks are simply explained by some event that seems to fit their color and shape, but these events certainly did not cause them.

What not to do and not to see and what to do and see

Birthmarks aside, in most cultures there are many things pregnant women should not do, or even see. Such prohibitions range from suggested advice to taboos. Violations invite trouble for the mother and/or the child, meted by the supernatural and some are punishable by the tribal authority. Most of these prohibitions have a valid foundation that is embellished with mystical folklore to reinforce its observation. But some are quite difficult to comprehend and even more difficult to justify. Maybe a more intensive study will find some rationality in some of the more bizarre practices. I will show the possible explanation for each custom wherever I can find it.

It makes a lot of sense that a Chinese expectant mother "should not frequent gossipers as these persons might disturb her repose" (*Chinese Medical Review*, 1852, in Sorel 1984, p. 24). It is less easy to explain why a woman in Madagascar should not wear a hat during pregnancy because this would make for a difficult delivery.

In Afghanistan, a native of that country said, a mother-to-be should not cut with scissors or use any sharp instrument because this would result in the baby's lips being cut. Leaving aside the doubtful consequences on the baby's lips, it certainly makes sense to tell women in advanced stages of pregnancy to be extremely careful with sharp instruments because they may not be as sure-footed as usual.

In the same vein, in Taiwan, pregnant women are not supposed to use a needle to sew as this too would harm the baby's lip. The mother-in-law will do all the sewing.

In many cultures pregnant women are kept from seeing an ugly or scary animal and sometimes they are excluded from seeing the slaughter of a large animal. The intent is always the same, keeping the woman away from sadness and ugliness, and especially from being frightened. Among the animals that a pregnant woman should avoid looking at are especially monkeys. In Jakarta, according to a native of that country, looking at a monkey will cause her child to become ugly.

In Brazil, seeing a snake during the first trimester of pregnancy might cause a woman to lose her child. In Zaire, looking at a certain bird could make the baby be born malformed. Malformation, in Indonesia, could be caused by eating pineapples during gestation.

How the environment can influence the child in the womb is not explained, but there are hardly any cultures that do not believe in such an influence. The theory in general is quite valid, as we now know for certain that the fetus can hear and sense light. Among all the talk about nature and nurture that goes on among psychologists and sociologists, the forgotten part is the baby's prenatal learning period, as explored over the last thirty years by the author (von Raffler-Engel 1964; 1989).

In many countries, pregnant women are encouraged to look at pretty things as this has a beneficial effect on the child. A Filipino woman attributed the handsome looks of her brother to her mother's watching movies with a particularly handsome actor.

Considerably more fascinating is the story about the brother of a Turkish woman. On the wall in their mother's home there was a picture of a blue-eyed man and her mother was fond of gazing at that picture. Although both parents had dark eyes, her brother has blue eyes and this woman attributed those unusual blue eyes to her mother's looking at that picture. Whether the woman who told that story really believed it herself I do not know, but she certainly assumed that her explanation could be acceptable.

Given the influence of just looking, caution may be recommended throughout. In Madagascar, a pregnant woman is careful to whom she may talk because, after a lengthy conversation, the child may come to resemble him. I forgot to ask whether the potential for resemblance equally applied to male and female conversation partners.

A friend of mine told me a true story that happened in Chicago some ten years ago. A white woman married to a white man bore a child of dark skin and Negro features. Her husband sued for divorce but the woman insisted that she had been a faithful wife. The non-Caucasian features of the child were due to "prenatal influence." One night she saw a Black man standing outside her bedroom window and this scared her tremendously. During the divorce proceedings, a professor of genetics from the University of Chicago was brought into court as an expert witness. He listened to the story and said that he had only one question: "Was the window closed or was it open?"

African-American mothers-to-be are not allowed to look at themselves. If they look into a mirror, their baby will become blind.

In central India, a pregnant woman avoids the shadow of a man because if it falls on her, the child could be born with the features of this stranger (Pedlow 1900, p. 60; in Frazer 1935, vol. 3, p. 82–83). It is always best not to stare at anything and it seems to me that sexual connotations do play a role in such harmful gazing. In El Salvador, looking at a cucumber could make the unborn child look like a vegetable.

We all know that if a black cat crosses the street on which we are walking or driving, this is said to bring bad luck. I have seen respectable businessmen stopping their car, then driving backwards a little bit before driving on as planned. I really expected to hear more about cats crossing the way when I did this survey, but similar stories were not mentioned. What comes closest to it is the superstition jokingly reported by a woman from Cuba. She told my then assistant Ms. Reynolds: "If you are pregnant riding in a car and meet another automobile with only one headlight, you must stop, get out and spit on the ground, or your baby will be crosseyed."

Personal care and clothing

Nowadays pregnant women are advised to keep good personal hygiene. Cleanliness on the person as well as in the home discourages parasites. That is quite obvious. In Japan, in order to have a pretty baby, pregnant women used to give the toilet an extra scrubbing every day. If this makes some sense, other customs are a bit hard to explain. Venezuelan women should not sweep their floors at night when they are with child. I cannot understand why they would do housekeeping chores at night even when not pregnant.

Speaking of household chores, nowhere are pregnant women supposed to move heavy objects. In Taiwan, neither the mother nor the father may move their furniture. But, for some strange reason, they are allowed to move their bed.

Coming back to personal hygiene, women's hair is the subject of many myths, and the period of pregnancy is particularly rich in such precepts. In Zaire, where women cut their hair in sign of mourning, during pregnancies they do not do this nor do they wear the black beads of mourning. Turkish women never cut their hair during pregnancy. In Venezuela, pregnant women are not supposed to cut another person's hair as this would damage that person's hair. One is reminded of the taboos associated with menstruation.

In many cultures pregnant women are discouraged from bathing or taking showers. How they keep clean is not explained. Black Americans may continue bathing, but if they hang their clothes to dry on the clothes line, their baby will strangle on its umbilical cord.

And now, coming to what is appropriate for pregnant women to wear. Here, again, the sensible is mixed with the bizarre. As said above, in Madagascar, the expectant mother must not wear a hat lest her delivery be very difficult (Ruud 1960, p. 241). Often the reasons given for doing or not doing certain things are odd, but the injunction per se is sensible. In this regard, however, I fail to understand why a pregnant woman should not protect her head from the hot sun.

Concerning the color of clothing, all makes lots of sense. Dark colors are avoided for women with children in several societies. Even in modern Europe, pregnant women are seldom seen dressed in black. Among the Hindus in India, as well as some Christian Peruvians and Czechs, even the fathers wear light-colored clothing when they come to receive the newborn. Americans dress their infants in light blue and baby pink. Cribs and children's rooms are decorated in soft colors. The clothing for the baby and anybody cuddling the baby in his/her arms as well as for the mother while she carries it is of great importance indeed. Dark colors may fade from sweat and affect the fetus through the mother's skin or the newborn in its father's arms.

Physical exertion

The details may vary, but all over the world a pregnant woman is to be treated kindly for the sake of her child. She is given help to lighten her daily load. The one exception to this rule I have encountered so far is among some tribes of American Indians where women are encouraged to work extra hard so that their baby will be born strong and healthy. Somehow modern society comes close to this idea when women are told to exert themselves so that their muscles will be trained for the heavy task of delivery and the oxygen flow to the fetus will be assured. The Japanese encourage a modicum of exercise to facilitate the delivery and to make sure the baby will have strong muscles.

What to eat and what not to eat

The folklore surrounding food is voluminous. Not all of it centers on nutritional benefits. Many prescriptions concern the emotional state of the mother-to-be. All cultures believe that it is not conducive to the well-being of the fetus if the mother is unhappy or emotionally disturbed.

Some foods conjure up a perturbing picture and the injunction to avoid them parallels the prohibition to attend funerals. In many countries pregnant women are not allowed to be present at the slaughter of large animals. In Madagascar the woman does not eat meat from a calf that has died during calving or was born prematurely. This might cause her to miscarry. Expectant mothers of the Zuni tribe of Native Americans refrain from eating the entrails of lamb as "this makes them think of eating their own baby."

In a less macabre vein, in Madagascar a pregnant woman must not eat ginger root because this root sometimes looks like deformed fingers or toes (Ruud 1960, p. 238). In another region of Madagascar, the woman must not eat fish lest her child might get a scaly skin. In Taiwan pregnant women limit their intake of soybeans because the baby's skin might become reddish. Black Americans limit their intake of starch because the baby might get white spots. In the Philippines, eating black beans will give a dark skin to the expected baby.

It is not only the looks of certain foods which conjure up negative connotations. Sometimes it is the name of a food item which is similar to something scary or unpleasant. Such food is then avoided by association.

In the North American culture, most dietary advice to pregnant women is solely based on its nutritional value even when it is phrased in flowery terms. In Utah, pregnant women are advised not to eat a potato with a spoiled spot (Hand 1976, p. 280). This really makes a lot of sense because damaged food is carcinogenic. Mormons are also advised to eat tomatoes as this will give rosy cheeks to their offspring (Hand 1976, p. 280). This is good advice because tomatoes are rich in vitamins that foster good blood circulation in the mother and, consequently, enrich the placenta.

In the mid-nineteen hundreds, American women were advised to eat little so that they would not gain too much weight and lose their graceful appearance as it is difficult to lose all of the weight gained during pregnancy. At that time the American culture was very little child-oriented. This has changed and gynecologists have come to recognize that the fetus needs a great deal of nourishment because of its rapid rate of growth, which causes many of the nutrients to be used up to form new tissues. If there is not enough nourishment via the placenta, the fetus grows at a slower rate and, at best, will be born underweight; at worse, it will be retarded. I do not know of any other culture where women were advised to

refrain from satisfying their normal desire for food during pregnancy. A social fad, like this one, is pretty much a form of superstition.

The advice for pregnant women to limit their food intake is contrary to the medically proven needs of the fetus (Perry 1990), but
other negative injunctions that, directly or indirectly, have to do
with food make pretty good sense, like the one reported by Fife
from Hyde Park, Utah, that said "the wife should not indulge her
husband while he is under the influence of alcohol, for idiocy or
other serious maladies are likely to be passed on to the child" (Fife
1976, p. 282).

When it comes to the actual intake of a modicum of alcohol,
cultures vary over time and space. In Italy expectant mothers are
"fortified" with the purest homemade wine. Equally contrary to
the opinion of most of my American respondents who advocate
teetotalism during pregnancy, Hippocrates (Hippocrates 1931,
Regimen in Health, VI, p. 53) advised that while children should
be given their wine "well diluted," "less diluted drinks are better
for the womb and for pregnancy." Hippocrates (Medicine, Section IV, Aphorism 1) also advises that "Drugs may be administered to pregnant women, if required, from the fourth to the
seventh month of gestation. After that period, the dose should be
less" (Lloyd 1978, p. 216, in Loomis 1948, p. 7).

Interviewing families about their culture's dietary concerns for
expectant mothers tends to produce more statements about what
these women should not eat than about what they should eat. Primarily, they mention the necessary avoidance of food items which,
when consumed in large amounts, are used to induce abortion.
For this reason, Brazilians warn against drinking strongly brewed
black tea and eating much black pepper.

In general, from India to the Americas, spicy food is discouraged because it could lead to miscarriage. It is also generally
advised not to eat pork. No specific reason is given and I assume
it is because this meat is more easily infected than other meats. In
India, pineapples are rejected because they might induce miscarriage. In Brazil the eating of large amounts of fruits with high acid
content is believed not only to give the woman a stomach ache,
but also to have the baby grow too much hair.

In Guatemala the list of food to be avoided is pretty long:
pineapple, melon, avocado, fresh cheese, pork and seafood. What

pregnant women should eat usually concerns either a "healthy diet" in general terms or specifics to make her feel comfortable. In El Salvador, green mangoes are eaten to combat morning sickness. But then there are strange rules. The Zunis are not allowed to eat deer meat when they are pregnant because if they do, they are likely to have twins. I do not know why the Zunis dislike twins, but many cultures have negative connotations about twins. What is, of course, most incomprehensible is how a woman pregnant with one child can conceive a second one by eating deer meat. There are instances of conceptions at a few months apart, but they are extremely rare.

Among Southern white rural Americans the conviction that if a pregnant woman does not get the food she craves, her baby will be harmed is no less universal than in any other part of the world. It is held by men as much as by women. I've already mentioned birthmarks. Another possible harm reported by a Native American woman is that the baby will be born with its mouth hanging open. When the woman gets what she craves, the child may still be affected. One Southern white rural American woman craved onions and her son "just loves onions." During her second pregnancy she craved watermelons and "her daughter always runs to the store to buy herself a watermelon." According to another woman of similar background, exactly the opposite will happen. If the mother did not satisfy her craving, the child will never want to eat that particular food.

In Brazil, if the woman does not get what she craves, she may have a difficult delivery or even lose her child. European fairy tales are full of stories about women craving certain foods. They have to be satisfied, even if it means for the husband to go into someone else's field and steal some fruit or vegetables. Satisfying a woman with child appears to take moral precedence, I assume because a life is at stake.

Among all reports on food cravings in the literature and from among the people interviewed for this book, the strangest craving was by a woman in the Philippines. She suddenly wanted to eat live mice. Her husband caught them for her and she ate them — alive.

Conclusion

I hope my readers enjoyed learning about the folktales from far away places. It was a rewarding experience for my son and myself to collect all those stories. The greatest reward is in how much understanding one gains from them about the nature of the embryo and the fetus. Knowledge comes from reading medical journals, but the real understanding comes from listening to the tales of old.

As early as ten and a half weeks of conceptual age, the palms of the fetus' hands are sensitive to touch and by fifteen to seventeen weeks, sensitivity has spread to the abdomen and buttocks. At eleven weeks the fetus can produce complex facial expressions and at twelve weeks it can close its fingers and thumbs and open its mouth in response to pressure applied to the thumb. The pregnant woman who touches her abdomen for the pleasure of feeling that she carries a baby inside can now feel a much greater pleasure knowing that the little one is capable of noticing her caresses. In olden times when she was listening to the tales of her people she already knew this. Then came modernization and disbelief, but now fetal research has provided her with the scientific proof she needed and she can freely follow her instincts without feeling backwardly superstitious.

Around the eighteenth week of gestation, the fetus has grown so strong that its mother can clearly feel its movements. This period is called the quickening and for most women it is the most exciting moment in their pregnancy. Among the women that were interviewed for this book, many women originally from the countryside described this sensation like "a message from the child to tell that it was there"; fewer urban women made such remarks.

Women who are ambivalent about having a child often develop a positive attitude after they feel the life within them. Some women, on the contrary, feel trapped even more than at the beginning of an unplanned pregnancy. But by far the majority of women do not undergo a voluntary abortion after the period of quickening. Many men too feel that after this period their mate should not undergo abortion. In many countries where abortion is legal, it is permitted only during the first trimester of gestation.

Why is quickening perceived as such a watershed? The instinctive reason is that the mother can feel the child moving and that traditional customs tell her that from that period on the fetus communicates with her, almost like a live child. The scientific reason is that at about that time, three months of conceptual age, slow brain activity can be registered with the use of electrodes. And when there is brain activity, there is enough consciousness to sense pain. The folktales speak mostly of pleasure. Obviously when pleasure can be felt, pain can be sensed too. Consciousness encompasses both.

Parents in Communist China may not know about the scientific proof of consciousness in the fetus after quickening, but they have a much stronger resentment when the official policy of "One family — one child" is enforced through abortion after the period of quickening. A woman who loses her child through miscarriage is filled with more poignant sadness if it happens after quickening than before. Doctors have noticed severe cases of depression. It is not that a bonding period of three months is that much more powerful than a slightly shorter bonding period. It is the loss of an interactive companionship which determines the degree of attachment and sadness in case of separation.

Folktales recognize the importance of quickening and deal with this event as extensively as with birth. A very old religion, like the Jewish one, also recognized quickening as the onset of conscious life. It is the tradition that a woman's first son must be dedicated to service in the temple. If the parents want to keep him for themselves, they must bring him to the priests and pay for his "redemption." If a woman has a miscarriage after three months, her subsequent son is not considered a "firstborn" and therefore does not have to be redeemed. If she has a miscarriage at an earlier time, the law of redemption applies to a son born afterwards.

After quickening the mental development of the fetus proceeds rather rapidly. Sometime between 32 and 35 weeks, the fetus begins to differentiate between wakefulness, active sleep, and quiet sleep. After 36–38 weeks of gestation, premature babies show EEG features that can be seen in full-term newborns. It is after this period that some premature births proved viable. Given the phenomenal advances of neonatal care, it is not to be excluded that one day babies born as early as five and a half months may grow up to become fully normal individuals. The old folktales did not anticipate such phenomenal medical advances. They do something that is in full accord with such a possibility when they attribute full reasoning power to the fetus.

What should the modern woman learn from all this, the folktales and the medical findings? She should do what comes instinctually. Only she can now do this with full consciousness. The early brain activity of the fetus should make us think that it is never too early to begin developing our children's intelligence.

All over the world women sing lullabies and nursery songs to their children and many sing soft melodies while their child is still in the womb. Some sing for their unborn child while many just sing for themselves. It is only during the last twenty years that music has become the conscious force of prenatal communication. In Japan and in Taiwan playing music and singing for the avowed purpose of being heard by the child in the womb is by now common practice. In the West this custom is not yet as widespread, but is steadily gaining followers among mothers and fathers. The receptivity of the fetus to musical tones is beyond question and is largely known to the young generation. Everybody seems to elaborate on what type of music is beneficial to the unborn and which one is not.

When a Chinese mother living in the United States was asked whether she believed she could make her child more intelligent or more musical by singing or reading while carrying it in her womb, she insisted on the benign effect of classical music. She reported that when she played rock 'n roll music, the child in her belly jumped and jerked "as if in protest" until she changed to classical music.

The merits of classical music over other forms of melodious tones may be in doubt. What is certain is that the unborn can distinguish between different types of musical sounds. In the late eighties, a consistent reaction to noise was observed in the fetus as early as 25 weeks of gestation. The absence of this startle effect is indicative of hearing deficits of the baby after birth. Subsequent bio-medical research has established that the sense of hearing is indeed formed in the fifth month. In a Swedish research project, pregnant women reported that they felt a kick immediately after a noise was heard. When they did not feel this reaction by their unborn, it was indicative that the fetus was not in good health. One is reminded of the folktale about the child in the womb which wanted to talk to its mother and to nobody else. The folk wisdom knew that the child in the womb is capable of distinguishing between different pitches.

Long before it became accepted knowledge that babies can hear before birth, the literature was full of tales of unborn babies moving rhythmically, or at least animatedly, when their mothers sat in a concert hall or wherever loud music was played. As is the case so often, folk wisdom preceded scientific validation. Now that science has validated the hunch that babies can hear before birth, mothers no longer must come out with awkward statements like the one we must all have heard: "I know it is not possible and it probably is coincidental, but my baby seems to move whenever I go to a concert."

In contrast to such disclaimers, an Indian woman from Peru said that she sang and played for all her children before birth because she knew that her babies were listening, that they "were all ears." This woman also believed that she could influence the intelligence and musical talents of her children by singing and talking to them while she carried them in her womb.

In the late eighties and the early nineties, I talked with many men and women from different countries and different social classes. They all seem to agree that the unborn child can hear and they believe the child's sensitivity to music can be enhanced by exposing it to good music before birth. Few among these same people, however, are convinced that talking or reading will increase the child's intelligence. This, they argue, should be done as soon as possible after the child is born. Among the Japanese I found a greater willingness to accept the idea that parental involvement in intellectual pursuits with their expected child can indeed foster its intelligence. I am reminded of the folktales where children who talked with their mothers were termed to be of great intelligence.

In the United States, among the educated young, everybody seems to know by now that women who listen to soap operas during their pregnancy, find out that after giving birth they can quiet their baby by humming the theme music of their favorite soap opera. The recognition of the musical sensitivity of the unborn has led young parents, mostly from the professional classes, to utilize musical themes like Linus' safety blanket for their baby. Some fathers prepare a tape recording to get their unborn child accustomed to a certain musical theme and then take this same recording to the delivery room so that the child finds something familiar when it enters this new world. One of these fathers, a medical doctor, was happy to see that when he played the recording, his newborn son turned his head and cast his eyes toward the source of the sound.

Of course, the sound the baby has heard most throughout his intra-uterine existence is that of its mother's voice. When a newborn is placed between two women who speak at the same time and the baby can hear them but cannot see them, it will turn its head toward the mother. Such information is now part of the training curriculum for neonatal nurses. I once lectured to such a group at Vanderbilt University and found the nurses quite receptive to my re-interpretation of the so-called old wives' tales.

There is still some discussion at what exact period the fetus reacts to external auditory stimuli. As said above, the scientifically proven time is 25 weeks of conceptual age. Some women who sing to their unborn have the impression that they are heard. To the people who asked me whether this is possible, I answered in the positive because there is more than one way to perceive musical sounds. Deaf people can dance to music because they feel the vibrations of the ground and in the air. A mother singing is also likely to move, ever so slightly, with the musical rhythm and the baby inside her might feel this.

Reading to the unborn child is less common by far. It is mainly practiced in Japan and to some extent in Taiwan. Of course, these parents do not believe that the unborn child can understand the words of what is read, but they feel it is important to get the child acquainted with the habit of being extensively read to so that it will be patient later on and listen and understand. In this sense, reading to the child in the womb helps to increase its intelligence by making it more receptive to learning. To have a scientific answer to this question we may have to wait and gather comparative data. Until then, I may be permitted to say that I am personally convinced that it helps and if it does not, it certainly can do no harm. So, let's keep reading.

I conducted a small survey among various groups to get an opinion on whether they believed that verbal communication and reading would increase the intelligence of a child when practiced before its birth. In Japan most people answer in the affirmative. In the United States some parents do not even believe they can communicate with the unborn while others told me that they do it because it is practiced in Japan and must have given good results because the Japanese are pretty intelligent. In Turkey, some upper class women dismiss the whole idea as backward, just like folktales. Other Turkish women of the same social class sing and talk and are convinced that the baby inside them can hear them. A woman from El Salvador who spoke and sang to her unborn said that in the lower strata of her country 60% of women were pregnant without marriage and too poor and too busy to even think about such matters.

A woman from Venezuela did not believe that talking and singing to the unborn would make the child more intelligent, but that such efforts must begin immediately after birth to stimulate the newborn's senses. In Brazil, talking and singing to expected children for the purpose of developing their intelligence is not a popular belief, but many women think that playing music when pregnant is a good thing and many women admit to talking to their unborn children by instinct, without any thought of doing anything beneficial for the child.

One becomes aware of how widespread the belief in prenatal communication is by now when one hears that a Somali woman went against her doctor's advice and did not sing to her unborn because she saw no purpose to this. On the other hand, a woman from Mozambique said she had never heard of developing a child's intelligence before birth and that it never crossed her mind to talk to a child she was carrying.

The other senses of the fetus develop later and, somehow, pregnant women seem less concerned about them as communication is enacted by touch and sound and these are the senses that develop earliest. The sense of taste appears between 34 and 39 weeks of gestation. Fetuses, like infants, have a preference for what tastes sweet. The sense of smell is documented only during the seventh month. The eye develops very gradually and only in the seventh month of gestation does it become sensitive to light.

The most important question this book wants to pose to its readers is at what time in the womb does learning begin. We know that the brain waves can be registered at a very early period. I have shown this in the chapter on medical evidence. At what time does volition begin? We do not know the exact time. What we know is that newborn babies have a willful personality of their own and that there are great individual differences. Given that the newborn expresses its needs so soon after birth, there must have been a period of development for such behavior previous to birth.

Some of the folktales and usages reported in this book seem awfully strange, some make a lot of sense, and some leave one undecided. Eventually, medical science may very well discover that they are all founded on solid principles. Of course, deep down, what we really care about is to find out what an expectant mother can do to make her baby healthy and intelligent.

Above all, she must make the baby feel welcome by listening to its movements and responding to them. She may also wish to get the unborn child accustomed to her singing and to instrumental music and, eventually, she may want to get the little one accustomed to the soft voice of its mother and the deep voice of its father reading aloud or reciting poems. By stimulating the sensory capabilities of the fetus we may help it to start developing to its fullest potential. Isn't this what all parents want?

From my perspective, all the superstitious usages and fairy tale-like stories are testimony to the perception of the fetus as a separate human being, likely to be influenced by the environment both hormonally through its mother and directly from the outside world. The fetus is an individual, a little person and not just a chunk of flesh inside its mother.

As I will show in the chapter on Enculturation later on, the child is part of its community even before it is born. Folklore knows this.

References

Acta Sanctorum (1643). Antwerp.

Adams, F.P. (1952). *The FPA book of quotations*. New York: Funk and Wagnall.

Alexander, H.B. (1920). The great gods, chapter II: Mexico, section IV. In Gray & Foote, *Latin American mythology* (vol. XI, pp. 57–71). New York: Cooper Square Publishers.

Apollodorus (1954). *The Library* (with an English translation by James George Frazer, vol. II, chapter 2, section 1). Cambridge, MA: Harvard University Press.

Bolte, J. & Polívka, G (revisors) (1963). Die klare Sonne bringt es an den Tag, Nr. 115. In *Anmerkungen zu den Kinder- u. Hausmärchen der Bruder Grimm* (vol. 2, pp. 531–535). Hildesheim: G. Olms.

Boyer (1607). Neuvermehrte heilsame Dreckapotheke.

Bushnell, J.H. (1947). Medical folklore from California. In *Western folklore* (vol. 6, pp. 273–275).

Callaway, H. (compiler and translator) (1868, reprinted 1970). *Nursery tales, traditions, and histories of the Zulus in their own words* (chapter Uhlakanyana, pp. 6–40). Springvale, Natal: J.A. Blair.

Carnoy, A.J. (1917). Tradition of the kings and Zoroaster. In Gray & Foote, *Iranian mythology* (vol. VI, chapter V, pp. 320–343 .

Castillo de Lucas, A. (1958). *Folkmedicina*. Madrid: Editorial Dossat.

Chamberlain, D. (1988). *Babies remember birth*. New York: Ballantine Books.

Chatelain, H. (compiler) (1894). Sudika-Mbambi. In *Folktales of Angola* (Memoirs of the American Folklore Society, vol. 1 chapter 4, section 5, pp. 85–96). Boston: Houghton Mifflin.

Durant, W. (1935). *The story of civilization. Part I. Our oriental heritage*. New York: Simon and Schuster.

English, H.B. & English, A.C. (1970). *A comprehensive dictionary of psychological and psychoanalytical terms*. New York: David McKay Co.

Erman, A. & Krebs, F. (1899). *Aus den Papyrus der königlichen Museen*. Berlin: B. Spemann.

Fife, A.E. (1976). Birthmarks and psychic imprinting of babies in Utah folk medicine. In W.D. Hand (Ed.), *American folk medicine: A symposium* (pp. 273–283) (held at the UCLA Conference on American Folk Medicine, 1973). Berkeley, CA: University of California Press.

Frazer, J.G. (1935). *The golden bough* (3rd ed.). New York: MacMillan.

Gray, L.H. & Moore, G.F. (Eds.). (1914–1932). *The mythology of all races* (13 vols.). Boston: Marshall Jones Co.

Hand, W.D. (1980). *Magical medicine: The folkloric component of medicine in the folk belief, custom, and ritual of the peoples of Europe and America*. Berkeley, CA: University of California Press.

Heller, B. (1930/1933). Arabische Motive in deutschen Märchen und Märchendichtungen. In J. Bolte & L. Mackensen (Eds.), *Handwörterbuch des deutschen Märchens* (Vol. 1, pp. 93–108). Berlin and Leipzig: Walter de Gruyter.

Hippocrates (1931). With an English translation by W.H. Jones. London: Heinemann and New York: Putman.

Kahlo, G. (1930/1933). Elementargedanken im Märchen. In J. Bolte & L. Mackensen (Eds.), *Handwörterbuch des deutschen Märchens* (pp. 519–524).Berlin and Leipzig: Walter de Gruyter.

Krappe, A.H. (1973). The myth of Balor with the evil eye and the Lay of Yonec. In *Balor with the evil eye: Studies in Celtic and French literature* (pp. 1–43). Norwood, PA: Norwood Edition.

Lloyd, G.E.R. (Ed.). (1978). *Hippocratic writings*. New York: Penguin Books.

Loomis, C.G. (1948). *White magic: an introduction to the folklore of Christian legends. Chapter 1: The Wonder Child* (pp. 15–26). Cambridge, MA: The Medieval Academy of America.

Macculloch, J.A. (1918). Paganism and christianity. In Gray and Foote (Eds.), *Celtic mythology* (Vol. 3, Chapter 15, pp. 206–213).

Metraux, A. (1948). The Tupinanmba In J.H. Steward (Ed.), *Handbook of South American Indians. Vol. 3: The tropical forest tribes* (pp. 95–133). Washington, DC: United States Government Printing Office.

Moss, L.W. & Cappannari, S.C. (1960). Folklore and medicine in an Italian village. *Journal of American Folklore, 73,* 95–102.

Patai, R. (1983). *On Jewish folklore*. Detroit: Wayne State University Press.

Paullini, C.F. (1714). *Neu-vermehrte heylsame Dreck-Apotheke*. Frankfurt am Mayn: Verlegung Friedrich Knochen und Söhne.

Pedlow, M.R. (1900). *Indian Antiquary, XXIX*.

Perry, P. (1990). Providing the chance of a lifetime. *Indiana Alumni, 53* (1), 26–29.

Plummer, C. (1910). *Vitae Sanctorum Hiberniae*. Oxford: Typographeo Clarendoniano.

Plutarch (1970). *De Iside et Osiride* (Edited with an introduction in English translation and commentary by J. Gwyn Griffiths). Cardiff: University of Wales Press.

Reischer, M. (1879). *Sefer Sha'are Y'rushalayim*. Warsaw.

Rivière, J. & Starkweather, C.C. (Transl.) (1901). Popular tales of the Kabyles. In *Moorish literature* (pp. 247–281). New York: Colonial Press (The World's Great Classics).

Ruud, J. (1960). *Taboo: A study of Malagasy customs and beliefs*. Oslo: Oslo University Press.

Shafer, S.M. (1988). Bilingual/bicultural education for Maori cultural preservation in New Zealand. *Journal of Multilingual and Multicultural Development, 9,* 487–501.

Shoemaker, H.W. (1927). *Scotch-Irish and English proverbs and sayings of the West Branch Valley of Central Pennsylvania*. Reading, PA: Reading Eagle Press.

Stein, M. (1985). *Te Wheke*. Gisborne, New Zealand: Gisborne Education Centre.

Sorel, N.C. (1984). *Ever since Eve*. New York: Oxford University Press.

Stucken, E. (1907). *Astralmythen* (5 vols. in 1 vol.). Leipzig: Eduard Pfeiffer.

Thompson, S. (1946). *The folktale*. New York: The Dryden Press.

Thompson, S. (compiler) (1929). *Tales of the North American Indians*. Bloomington, IN: Indiana University Press.

von Raffler-Engel, W. (1964). *Il prelinguaggio infantile.* Brescia, Italy: Paideia (Studi grammaticali e linguistici 5).

von Raffler-Engel, W. (1991). The contribution of psycholinguistics to the study of language origins. In B. Chiarelli et al. (Eds.), *Language origins: A multidisciplinary approach* (pp. 183–193) (Proceedings of the NATO Advanced Studies Institute, Cortona, Italy, 1988). Dordrecht: Kluwer Academic Publishers (NATO AS series).

Werner, A. (1925). Heroes In Gray and Foote (Eds.), *African mythology* (Vol. 6, Chapter 6, pp. 213–224).

Winick, C. (1977). *Dictionary of anthropology.* Totowa, NJ: Littlefield, Adams & Co.

Fertility Propitiatory Rites

Introduction

My readers may wonder why a linguist is interested in fertility rites. My book deals with this theme not only as a sequel to the chapter on superstitions surrounding the pregnant woman and her unborn child. Logically, this chapter on the pre-conceptual period should precede the chapter dealing with the period before conception.

The emphasis of the book is on *taikyó* which is practiced only during gestation. It should, nevertheless, be mentioned that there are many practices which are performed before conception. How such practices influence the health of the child that eventually will be conceived is difficult to determine. One thing, so far, that seems to be certain is that unwanted children have more problems later in life than children that are either wanted or unplanned but happily accepted. We are not only talking of problems of child neglect, but of the much more subtle consequences of psychological problems later in life even when such children are reasonably cared for during infancy.

That quitting to smoke and adopting healthy eating habits by parents who plan to have a child are beneficial practices is obvious. Whether any eating habits can influence the sex of the child is not as clear. In any case, the subject of sex determination will be dealt with in the subsequent chapter. It is doubtful that women who are pregnant against their desire will practice *taikyó* as they should unless, as often happens, they end up happily accepting their condition.

Even in a planned pregnancy, a woman can practice *taikyó* with love and enthusiasm or she can engage in it dutifully without enchantment because it is the thing to do, just as she got pregnant because her husband wants a son.

Language development in the infant is enhanced by the mother's communication with this child before its birth and a much desired child is likely to receive more such attention from both of its parents. It is certain that a child is greatly desired when its parents have undergone the expensive and complicated medical treatments for infertile couples available today, just as when in the past or in less medically advanced countries, couples underwent the elaborate rituals designed to assure fertility.

But there is more than all this to explain why a linguist might be interested in exploring what people do to make sure that they have children. Language represents power. Throughout history, the victor has often imposed his language on the vanquished. This happened when the German speaking South Tyrol was annexed to Italy after World War II. The courts were not allowed to hear cases presented in any language but Italian and this left the local population largely without justice. This happened in the United States when the children of Native Americans were separated from their parents and sent to boarding schools where English was the only language spoken. When the descendants of the French settlers of the province of Quebec wanted independence from Canada, what they stressed most was the use of their native language as opposed to the English of their conquerors.

The loss of language signifies the loss of power and a family becomes extinct when it no longer produces children. The ancestors are forgotten without descendants to remember them. Language, as can be seen from the Quebeckers and similar groups, represents self and children represent the continuation of self. A linguist can see a parallel between an immigrant group preserving its language and people doing everything they can to assure their progeny.

Most societies assure the survival of the group through procreation. The exception was a sect of the Pennsylvania Quakers who practiced celibacy and planned to perpetuate their society by means of proselyzing. This method worked for a short period only and by now the sect has become extinct.

Attitudes toward infertility

As far as I know, these Quakers are the only group where every member abstained from sexual intercourse. There are societies which highly value celibacy in a segment of their population, Catholic and Buddhist nuns and priests among them.

In other religions, such as Judaism, it is a father's duty to "teach his son to read and write and to find a good husband for his daughter." All males are obligated to follow the Biblical injunction to "be fertile and multiply" (Genesis I, 28 & IX, 1). This injunction is considered of such importance that it is the only one which is explicitly given twice. When a Jewish couple is unable to have a child after five years of marriage, they are supposed to move to Jerusalem. Living in their ancestral holy city is believed to facilitate conception. If after ten years of marriage, they are still childless, traditional Jews feel compelled to dissolve their marriage and try other partners. But before taking such a drastic step, they will try every imaginable remedy. Most well known is the practice of drinking an infusion prepared with the grass that grows in the slits between the stones of the Western Wall, the last remnant of the holy temple (Reischer 1879, p. 91–92, in Patai 1983, p. 347).

Catholics seek the intervention of a special saint, the Franciscan monk St. Anthony of Padua. In the churches of Italy one can see young women as well as worried mothers-in-law kneeling in front of his statue and burning candles to invoke his assistance. So far, I have never seen a father, probably because few men would admit to be the cause of childlessness.

In Japan, barren couples go to pray at the Shinto shrine of the god of fertility. The symbol of this god is a stone shaped like a penis. The decision of some modern Japanese women to remain childless is a recent trend that shocks many traditional Japanese as it goes counter to their culture. The government is concerned about the diminishing work force.

Since women increased their level of education and entered the professional work force, Germany and Japan have reduced the number of their children to the point they no longer will maintain their current level of population. As this becomes known, voices are heard in these countries strongly urging their women to have more babies. In Japan someone even suggested curtailing college education for females.

I have researched the folklore of mother and child for more than thirty years and have never encountered a culture which did not agree with the ancient Romans that a woman's children are her most precious jewels. The recent preference of some couples in the industrialized world to remain childless is a new phenomenon. Considering the current rush to maternity, it does not even seem to be a lasting phenomenon.

The fact is that few persons, if any, want to be childless. Many people want to limit the number of their children or have them at an opportune time. The proper timing for the birth of one's children is generally an individual decision, but it is also related to the whole of society.

Some African tribes and some American Indians practice infanticide in times of famine. There are South American Indian tribes who restrict the number of their children to what is considered the optimal size for the well being of the group. When an increase in population would exceed the pre-established size, they practice birth control by having their women drink certain herbal infusions. All these are temporary measures and in no way go counter to the basic desire to perpetuate the tribe.

The exception seems to be the Papuans who live in constant shortage of food. Abortion is practiced on a large scale and the women believe that "children are cumbersome" (Durant 1935, p. 50).

Among the men and women who choose to be sterilized, few want to be childless. Most wish to limit the number of children to those they already have. Even dictatorial regimes, such as the People's Republic of China, do not forcibly sterilize their citizens before they have at least one child. There appear to be exceptional cases, according to reports from India, where the government imposes indiscriminate mass sterilization. It is known that the people themselves abhor the practice.

All this shows how strong an instinct the desire for procreation is. The desire for sex is also a strong human urge, but the two are not necessarily felt to be tied together. As a woman from Mozambique put it, were it not for the wish to have children, no man would marry. A fascinating case of combining fertility with worry-free sex is reported for the men living before the Biblical deluge.

Those men took two wives, one of whom produced their offspring while the other drank a contraceptive solution and behaved like a harlot (Patai, p. 425).

As my readers will see from the customs described in the following pages, people will go to great lengths and spend considerable amounts of money to fulfill their desire for children. In general, most cultures pity a woman who cannot bear a child. Among the Native Americans of the Amazon, a barren woman is looked down upon, particularly if she is the wife of a tribal leader. In Italy, unless she is a nun, an infertile woman had to bear the brunt of insults and cruel jokes. In East Africa, when a childless woman dies, her body is thrown away in the forest or another place where the land is never cultivated for fear that her ghost will make the earth infertile. As much as men must protect their country, women need to perpetuate its inhabitants. In Madagascar, pregnancy is called "the ancestors' continuation."

The Welsh have a proverb from the sixteenth century which refers to a woman with a big belly as one of the handsomest sights in the world. The Maori of New Zealand have the same word, "whenua," for land and placenta. The land offers the same feeling of warmth, belonging, security and sustenance to its people that the placenta offers to the fetus.

There is a natural bond between our own fertility and all of nature. At the end of the seventh month of gestation, the Hindu woman goes to the temple where the priests perform the appropriate rituals. She is dressed in green and wears green jewelry, like jades and emeralds. She will give some pieces of her clothing to her friends and relatives who are all invited for the ceremony. She is given fruit to eat. The symbolism associates her fruitfulness with that of the earth and her friends rejoice with her. Pregnant women never wear black among Brahmins. It is an inauspicious color, like withered leaves.

When barrenness is incurable, it is sometimes believed to be the result of sin. Among a Pennsylvania Dutch family, the barrenness of one daughter and the stillbirth of the only child of another daughter were attributed to their worldliness and their refusal to join the Dunkard church of their parents. It is often believed that abortion may be punished by the woman's inability to have a child later when she wants one. This belief is especially prevalent among Catholics for whom abortion is a grave sin.

Among the Scotch-Irish of Pennsylvania the sin of trying to abort a fetus is believed to be passed on to that very child if it survives the attempt and it may be born blind. Miscarriage, on the other hand, is often attributed to external forces. In many parts of the world and especially in Southern Europe, pregnant women beware of the evil eye.

Catholic priests and nuns, who make a vow of celibacy, are addressed as "Father" and "Mother." Not being allowed to have children of their own, they are considered the spiritual parents of their flock. This takes away the stigma of being childless and also absolves them from not obeying the Biblical injunction to "be fruitful and multiply."

Buddhists also have monks and nuns. The Buddha himself left his wife and children to fully devote himself to preaching. Of course, the Biblical injunction does not apply to Buddhism, but, interestingly, these celibate religious leaders also carry a title similar to "Father" and "Mother." The nations where Buddhism is practiced, like all other nations of which we have knowledge, consider it the function of a woman to bear children. A barren woman is disgraced. I turned up much less information concerning sterile men.

Social workers in the United States say that one of the obstacles to convincing young males of the black underclass to use condoms is that getting a girl pregnant is considered a show of machismo. For a poor girl, having a child is felt like entering adulthood. The first duty of the wife of a European crown prince as well as of the wife of a tribal chieftain is to provide an heir. Some of us remember when Farah Diba, wife of the shah of Persia, was repudiated in favor of a fertile queen.

In Muslim societies the status of a married woman is lowered if she remains childless. It is tacitly assumed that the failure to conceive is the woman's fault, a Muslim woman said, even when it is certain that "the husband has the problem."

In Sao Paolo, Brazil, the attitude seems to be more equitable. Both applicants for a marriage license, in addition to the usual Wassermann, are also tested for fertility. In all of Brazil, failure to have children after a certain number of years of marriage constitutes legal grounds for divorce.

In the Alps of Southern Germany and Austria, until about three generations ago, it was customary for couples to marry only after the girl had proved that she was fertile. As soon as she was pregnant, the boy took her to church for the big wedding ceremony. The virginal white dress was denied a girl only when she did not marry the first man who seduced her.

Folkloric practices to gain fertility

Given that the desire to have children is strong on both the individual as well as the social level, what do people do to combat infertility? Medical practices are well known. In this book, I want to present folk usages and beliefs. In his interviews, my son collected stories from around the world that have to do with fertility rites. I also found many such stories in the books I consulted. Here I do not only want to share information on these practices that sometimes are truly bizarre. What I want to share with my readers is also the faith people had throughout the ages that something can be done to make them fertile, a wish medical science has been able to fulfill only in the latter part of this century.

Getting fertility drugs or very complex treatments to facilitate conception is not only demanding but can also be very expensive. Even people of modest means make an effort to come up with the necessary financial coverage. This is not different from the willingness of earlier couples to go to the witch doctor who sometimes lived in far away places and who charged dearly for his or her incantations.

Food does not seem to play a role in today's sophisticated treatments of sterility, but in ancient times there were many foods women were either to eat or to avoid in order to combat sterility. Still, today, throughout East Asia men believe that drinking the hot blood of a snake right after it is killed will increase their potency. In the European countryside women prepare certain herbal teas to become more susceptible to impregnation. In several societies across the globe, barren women are said to gain fertility by eating earth or drinking water mixed with dirt. But, basically, nowadays couples unable to conceive go to a clinic and follow medical instructions which are getting more and more refined and promising of success.

Of course, in remote areas there are no such clinics and not all people know about the advances of modern medical science. I will now retell some of the usages infertile couples practice in their quest for progeny. I will bring these practices to the attention of my readers not to satisfy their curiosity about the outlandish customs of other populations, but to show the universal symbolism underlying even some of the most bizarre practices. Let's not forget that all the diverse human races share interfecundity. All peoples throughout history had statuettes symbolizing fertility (for some of these see Cottrell 1989, indexed under "Fertility"). Excavations everywhere unearth statues of a goddess of fertility.

I already mentioned the earth from which we all draw our sustenance as a universal symbol of fertility. Water, without which the earth could not produce our nourishment, is another such symbol. Water is frequently combined with the moon. As the duration and the structure of the phases of the moon are like those of the menstrual cycle it seems natural that the moon plays a large part in fertility rites all over the world. The moon also governs the fertility of the earth and farmers everywhere watch for the moon for their planting seasons.

In Central Europe, a woman who has difficulty conceiving would expose the lower part of her body to the moon's rays when it is in the first or in the last quarter. I do not know whether this custom is still observed nowadays, but the belief that the moon governs fertility is still strong. It may be noted that this custom was particularly prevalent in Germany where the word for moon is masculine, as it is in Japanese. In Italian the word for moon is feminine. In some religious paintings the moon is associated with the cult of the Madonna who is venerated as the mother of all.

In the Amazon region of Brazil, women who wish to conceive go to the river during the full moon. A virgin may also go to the river at those times and become pregnant by one of the pink dolphins that swim in the waters. When the dolphin spots a young woman he puts on a hat so as not to show what he really looks like. He then seduces the girl like a real man. In the small villages along the Amazon river there are many stories about the pink dolphin. No social stigma is attached to the woman or the child she bears from this union.

A similar story in Japan has a less benign ending. The flat-headed kappa is a water spirit who loves to drink sake and to

chase unwary women and impregnate them. According to one author, as recently as fifty years ago, babies born of such unions were
often burned to death (Helm 1991). The kappa is not a benign
spirit, but he is extremely polite and this makes it possible to
defend oneself. His head is flat because it has to hold a container
filled with water. If one bows very deferentially and very low to
him, he feels compelled to reciprocate with the same polite bow
and the water will fall out and he loses his strength. Escape then
is easy.

The most obvious symbols of fertility take the shape of the male
organ. I already mentioned the Shinto god of fertility. In Brittany,
all megaliths have figured in ancient folk rituals, many of them
associated with fertility. In one locality, "women hoping to become pregnant used to raise their skirts to the dolmen at full
moon." During the first night of May, maidens "would sneak out
and slide bare-bottomed down the huge fallen stones." Also at full
moon, childless couples would visit another menhir, "both completely naked, and the husband would chase the wife around the
stone, while their parents, behind another menhir, acted as look-
outs" (Robert 1989, p. 152).

The shape of a plant or the looks of fruit and vegetables may
also be suggestive of the act of procreation. What ancient people
knew all along and what Western culture is rediscovering only
now is the inseparability of mind and body. For a specialist in nonverbal behavior, like myself, the folk practices I am going to recount below are one more example of how concrete language and
imagery can be separated only as an artifact of the analysis.

And now, after all this philosophizing, let's go back to the de-
scription of what people do to propitiate fertility. The Native
American Mescalero Apache take the pollen from the cattail plant
and sprinkle it on the heads of young girls during puberty rites to
ensure that they will be fertile when they get married.

For the Native American Zunis, grinding corn could make a
woman conceive, albeit not a virgin. One of the many kind people
who helped me collect pertinent information while I was writing
this book told me of a Zuni woman who was a physician and
doubted the practice of her people. This young woman went to
witness the corn grinding only out of curiosity. But while watching
she got so involved that she went down to the floor herself and
participated in the grinding. Soon thereafter she discovered that

she was pregnant. After this experience she no longer doubted the wisdom of her tribe.

In Europe and the Americas, newlyweds leaving the marriage ceremony are showered with rice or birdseed. Nowadays their friends simply shout wishes for a happy life together. Not too long ago these wishes for a happy marriage included the wish for healthy children. The Italians used to wish for "figli maschi in quantità" (many male children).

Hippocrates suggested a strange test to see whether the infertility was due to the woman or her husband. "If a woman does not conceive, and you wish to know if she can conceive, cover her with wraps and burn perfumes underneath. If the smell seems to pass through the body to the mouth and to the nostrils, be assured that the woman is not barren because of a physical deficiency of her own."

Hippocrates is to be commended because the general assumption throughout seems to be that infertility is the woman's fault. Until quite recently, throughout the Western world, when a couple went to the doctor because they could not conceive, the woman was tested before the man. No other partners are tested at the same time.

Some women conceive but have difficulty carrying the baby to term. Research in these last few years has discovered that the fault may lie with the fathers when men work in factories where they are exposed to harmful chemicals (Richards 1989).

In the previous chapter where I reported on the customs designed to keep a pregnant woman contented and her baby safe, my readers may have observed that all customs refer only to the woman. Beyond a drunken father, the recognition that the health of the father definitely affects the capacity for life of the fetus is only of very recent date.

Adoption

Reproductive problems are often complex and persistent, but fortunately, in our times, medical science has advanced greatly and is helping many infertile couples to become parents. For those whom medicine cannot help or who, for religious reasons, object to the necessary practices, there remains the option to adopt.

Children give joy, whether biologically born to their parents or only raised by them with loving care. In Liberia, when a woman has difficulty conceiving, she is told to relax and play with the fertility doll. If she does not become pregnant, it is not considered a tragedy. She will simply ask a friend who has many children to give one of them to her. That child then has two loving mothers.

One Liberian mother, who is a friend of my son's has two children but wants more. So, her sister who conceives very easily and already has many children, becomes pregnant again. The child she is carrying is eagerly awaited by both sisters, the biological mother and the one who will take care of the baby as soon as it is born. The sex of the baby does not matter. There are no official adoptions in Liberia, but no couple is left childless. In the same spirit, if a family has difficulty supporting all of their children, another, better situated family will take care of raising some of these children as their own.

In ancient Rome, among prominent families, adoption to help out a friend with no heir was common practice. The adoptee carried both family names. Similar customs prevailed among the aristocracy in old-time Europe. These types of adoptions are coming into use again among the American middle classes and are termed "open adoptions."

This is not the place to describe all types of adoptions and the legal implications in the different countries of the world. All I want to bring out here is that the adoptive parents should be extra kind to their new ward. Their new child has lived for nine months in a different environment, in the womb of a mother who had a different voice and a different body rhythm from the mother who holds it now in her loving arms. Awareness of the surroundings does not begin only at birth but before, in utero.

Conclusion

The theme of my book is *taikyō*. This chapter shows that when a mother speaks to the child in her womb she is not alone. Her warm feelings are shared by her proud husband and their entire community. She represents "the continuation of the ancestors." For a linguist it is fascinating to study the words various cultures have for the maternal womb. The womb is compared to "the earth" where all human beings live and from which we obtain our sustenance.

References

Cottrell, A. (1989). *The MacMillan illustrated encyclopedia of myths and legends*. New York: MacMillan.

Helm, L. (1991). In Japan, it's time to celebrate the dead. *Los Angeles Times*, Aug. 31, p. 8 (A).

Patai, R. (1983). *On Jewish folklore*. Detroit: Wayne State University Press.

Richards, B. (1989). Fathers' chemical contacts linked to pregnancy woes. *The Wall Street Journal*, July 6, p. B1.

Roberts, D. (1989). Tantalizing to scholars and tourists, Carnac's megaliths remain an enigma. *Smithsonian, 20*, No. 6 (September), 146–159.

How to Determine the Sex of the Child in the Womb

Folk Beliefs on How to Influence the Sex of the Child Before Conception and Clues on How to Recognize Whether it is a Boy or a Girl Growing in the Womb

Introduction

As much as I enjoyed researching the topics for the preceding chapters, while going through the literature and interviewing people on the subject of the unborn child's sex, there were moments I felt sad. Throughout the centuries, and even today, the preference for a male heir can be tantamount with the suppression of the female. It can go as far as the degradation of the mother and the murder of the child.

Of course, such cruel behavior is not always the norm. What appears doubtful to me after going through the literature and talking with people, is that parents are frankly curious about what sex their child will be. I am inclined to believe that what most people really want to know is whether their child is male.

When looking at the questionnaire I designed, the reader will find one question asking whether the respondent wanted his/her first child to be a son. The people that were interviewed in person were asked this same question. The overwhelming majority of respondents, regardless of their country of origin, answered that they wanted their first child to be male. One father, after writing "yes," added "of course."

Finally, while analyzing the written questionnaires, I came across a different answer and I smiled, but much too early. The respondent, a man from Cambodia, wanted his first child to be a girl and he even gave a reason for his choice: "Because babies need lots of care, and if my first child were a girl, she could assist my wife later on when she bore my son, who then would get the best possible care."

The most unexpected statement came from a Zulu woman from South Africa. She would have a burial for a miscarried fetus but only after she could "see whether it was a boy" (This information was obtained by my then assistant, Ms. Reynolds).

Among the people I interviewed in person, one middle class American father said that, although he feels embarrassed about this, in all honesty, he must tell me that, yes, he had wanted his firstborn to be a son. This was some twenty years ago. If his wife were pregnant now for the first time, he might not wish so strongly for a boy because in these past years he had come to realize the value of women to be equal to men.

Indeed, among the younger generation I found a couple of answers like this one: "It really does not matter, as long as the child is healthy." For a linguist, the change of attitude is quite interesting. In official documents in the United States of America, the language has been adjusted to become sex-neuter. In official lingo, "the language has been desexed." A policeman has become a police officer, the mailman is now a mail carrier, and university catalogs no longer describe all medical students as "he" and all students in nursing as "she." In Japanese dictionaries, our favorite word, *taikyó*, is now defined as "an expecting mother's practice of something for having a good baby, either boy or girl" (Prof. Keiko Ikegami, personal communication). But not everybody is quite so modern. A man from Nigeria who was studying in the United States told me quite simply that he was going to get himself a good wife and "a good wife produces only sons."

People do not only want children, they would like them tailor-made in the sex of their choice. As the natural way of having children does not allow for such a choice, wishful thinking has created many folksy practices to assure that one's offspring will fulfill one's wishes. There are now medical procedures to select the sex of a child, but not everybody considers them ethical or wants to submit to them, or even knows about them. Once a woman is pregnant, there are new tests to show the sex of the child in the womb which involve only minimal risk. For many people these too are controversial.

In normal intercourse there is absolutely no way to influence this development. What has puzzled scholars over the centuries is that the male and the female populations are pretty much equal in number. What governs this distribution is totally unknown and we don't even have a clue for initiating research. There is no folk explanation for this phenomenon. And really there is no great curiosity about it among the masses. As we said, there is a natural curiosity to find out of what sex one's child will be. Consequently, many folktales have developed. These I want to share with you.

Reasons for the preference for a male child

The manifest desire for a male child has deep cultural-religious roots and there, frankly, is no evil in wanting a son. What we should all hope for is a change in the negative attitude toward a woman who keeps bearing daughters in societies that do not understand, or refuse to acknowledge, the fact that the sex of the child is determined by the father. Even those who know that the male embryo has one X chromosome and one Y chromosome while the female embryo has two X chromosomes often ignore that this combination is due to the paternal sperm.

Before describing the folk advice on how to beget a male child and the folk practices on how to influence the sex of the child after it has been conceived — which is truly impossible — I will present the reader with some of the cultural-religious tenets that require male descendants.

Except for couples who already have a male offspring, to get a male child is the prime desire of most.

The desire for a male descendant is especially strong in countries like China, where a son is the only guarantee for the continuation of ancestor worship, including the cult for the parents themselves when their time comes. In many parts of the world, there exists the belief that, at death, when the body decomposes, the spirit will linger on. The spirit of the dead is part of his family, just as when he was alive. He now influences the well-being of his descendants, watches over the crops and makes sure that his heir is fertile in producing a son of his own. On the part of the living, respect requires that they not forget their deceased ancestors who like to be remembered in thought and even with the pouring of an occasional libation. The latter is a gesture, not literally believed to be consumed by the dead. It is the duty of the first-born son to take care of the needs of the ancestral spirits.

In present-day Communist China abortion is compulsory after the birth of the first child. I taught in China and spoke with many people there and to Chinese living abroad. I have never met a woman who liked the idea of having to abort, whether the child she already had was a girl or a boy. I am told that in the Chinese countryside the population feels even more strongly that they should not be compelled to limit their births. They do not only cling to the traditional belief that having many children is a blessing, but, by growing their own food, they also have the capability of feeding their offspring. The children can also help with the work in the field. It is also somewhat more difficult to control the population in the vast countryside than in the cities. I am told that the government is a little more lenient toward farmers who want more than one child because they can feed the additional child and it is thus more difficult to force them to abort a second child with the threat of leaving the first one to starve and without adequate schooling.

When do people protest most to compulsory abortions and sterilizations? When their only child is a girl. In China, by now some families have been so successfully weaned from tradition that they are willing to restrict the number of their offspring to the governmentally authorized single child — provided that this child is a boy. They feel they must be allowed having children, any number of them, until they give birth to a male (Kirstoff 1990).

In the Chinese countryside, girls are sometimes put to death so that the family may preserve the right to have another child which it is hoped will be a boy. For many years there was no official penalty for such killings, but about five years ago a penalty of seven years in prison was imposed. Even so, law enforcement, I am told, is not rigorous. The communist government does not have a particular bias against females. Children of either sex may be destroyed at birth by stuffing gauze into their mouth or injecting alcohol into their fontanelle (Kirkwood 1990).

Earlier in this section I mentioned ancestor worship. This is a common term but, in many instances, it is not an accurate term. Mostly, what people do is honor the memory of the departed as a form of respect for one's elders and a means of keeping the family together. For Shintoism in Japan, each soul is created at the moment of conception. It survives the death of the body and goes to paradise, immediately or after a period of purgatory. Thus, all ancestors are in a spiritual existence and should be worshipped. Confucians in Japan as well as in China practice ancestor worship as a form of filial duty.

A Jewish son will burn a candle every year on the anniversary of his father's death and he will do the same on the death date of his mother, calculated by the lunar calendar. He does this in his home and there often will be a special service in his house of worship with the friends of his parents as well as his own. If the children of deceased parents do not live in the same locality and cannot easily get together, they will each honor their parents separately. If they can get together, the candle is lit by the oldest son.

The Japanese prepare libations for the departed at the site of the household shrine. There too the oldest son is in charge of the ceremony.

In Africa, the animists have banquets to honor the dead. The custom prevails even after some animists have converted to Christianity.

The ancient Romans kept statuettes of the "manes," their ancestors in their homes. In ancient Greece, legend even has it that, when a man was unable to make his wife conceive, one of his ancestors briefly took his form and impregnated her.

In modern traditional societies, like most of South America, it is felt that if there are girls, a brother is needed to protect them against other males. A house also needs a man to keep it in good condition and when the parents are old, they will need the support only a son can provide. In some parts of South America a man is not blamed for going with another woman if his wife keeps giving him only daughters.

Many South American families wait until they have a son before they start using birth control. The traditional attitudes persist in the countryside, but are changing in the cities where birth control is practiced even before the birth of a male child.

The desire for male descendants is universal reaching far beyond the countries where women are looked down upon when they produce only daughters. Fortunately, even though the desire for a male heir remains, the lack of appreciation for female children is lessening. In pre-World War II Japan, a woman was despised if she did not do the honorable thing of giving birth to a son. In our present time this attitude has changed very much in Japan where the old prejudice is explained historically. The shogun needed to have a son lest his family lose the power to rule. The prejudice eventually spread to the lower classes and they too wanted a male child.

Among the Kurds, the majority of whom are Muslim, every father wants his first-born to be a male. In any case, whenever he is born, the first son has an exalted position and is his father's favorite. He will inherit the family farm and keep the family name honored in the village. When his father dies, he will be responsible for his mother's welfare. The more sons a woman bears, the prouder she will be.

Sadly enough, almost everywhere, a woman's worth is determined not by the number of her children or how well she rears them, but by the number of sons she bears for her husband and his family.

The male as protector of his father in old age, of his mother in widowhood, and of his sisters' honor was repeatedly mentioned by respondents from Brazil. The importance of the male descendant is felt most poignantly in the villages where a man is needed to take care of the house and frequently also of the small farming land. An older brother is also needed to make the necessary marriage arrangements when a sister is pregnant out of wedlock.

In some parts of Brazil a woman is stigmatized if she remains childless, but there are two extenuating circumstances. If it is known that the problem stems from her husband, nobody talks about the lack of children; or if she is really outstanding in her profession, she will not be ostracized for being childless. This is the rare instance where I heard that a woman's worth can be measured by something other than her sons.

Most of India is Westernized and the practice of polygamy has largely been discontinued except when a wife does not produce a son. Then the man, with the encouragement of his family, acquires a second wife. This often is the benign solution. It may also happen that the wife is beaten up by the husband and his family and often quite beaten to death. She certainly is looked down upon by the community. I am told that this even happens in Indian families that have immigrated to the United States of America.

In India, amniocentesis is accepted practice and female fetuses are aborted, supposedly as an act of kindness to spare them the hard life of a woman that would be their fate were they to be born, not to mention the unnecessary burden they would impose on their parents. "It's better for an unwanted girl not to be born than suffer later" (McGowan 1989).

Until recently, among some Eskimo tribes, if the firstborn was female, the newborn girl was immediately carried outside the igloo to freeze to death. This was done very rapidly so that the mother might be spared added grief if she touched the child.

Some Indian tribes killed half their offspring, some allowed only a boy and a girl per family (Durant 1935, p. 50). There are also many superstitions that commanded the killing of the newborn (Ibid.). From the lowest classes to the highly educated, in India, only boys enjoy elevated status. Among the Brahmins it is felt that a male descendant is needed to carry on the family name. In some parts of India, live births of girls are considered unfortunate accidents and the newborns are hastily put to death.

In parts of Arabia, until not too long ago, female children were sometimes suffocated in the desert sand. In pre-Muslim Arabia, girls were sacrificed to the gods (Durant 1935, p. 291). The Kurds are ferocious warriors but very gentle family people. Abortion is unacceptable except when the mother's life is at stake. Infanticide is not generally practiced. Should a man kill his infant daughter it is believed that he became temporarily insane from the sorrow of not getting the much expected son. The act itself is abhorred.

In Korea, the year of the horse is believed to be inauspicious for girls. Nineteen-hundred and ninety was such a year and if sex tests showed a female fetus, an increase in abortions was expected. Girls born in the year of the horse are said to be "headstrong, intelligent, active, impatient and argumentative — not good marriage material."

In the United States, amniocentesis is usually requested to detect possible health defects. Sometimes, however, it is performed out of curiosity about the sex of the fetus. Even though recorded cases are infrequent, there are instances where the "wrong" sex is aborted; and the undesired sex is more often female than male (Leo 1989). Abortions solicited after these sex selection tests can be considered the modern equivalent of female infanticide. The so-called civilized world has different means from the so-called primitive Third World, but the goals are the same.

Folk practices to influence the sex of the child

Given that almost everyone seems to prefer a son, it is surprising that I did not come across more advice on how to assure a male birth, apart from praying to heaven for one, a practice common to most religions. The Mormons are the exception in their belief that wishing too strongly for a child of a specific sex is an usurpation of a prerogative belonging to God (Hand 1976, p. 282).

The Jewish religion does not allow for "vain prayers," meaning to ask for what is against the laws of nature. Such would be praying for a male child after the woman has conceived and the sex of the child has been irrevocably established (Babylonian Talmud 1965, Berachot IX, Mishna 3, p. 54A).

The Brahmins of India perform certain practices and direct their prayers to particular deities and make vows under a worship tree to ensure the birth of a boy.

On the secular side, over three hundred years before the common era, the Greek physician Hippocrates made a suggestion to men wishing to beget a male child. I doubt many men followed his advise, and even if they followed it, I doubt it would produce the desired boy, or even a girl, for that matter. The good physician prescribed that men tie up their left testicle as tight as bearable before engaging in intercourse (Sorel 1984, Introduction, p. XV).

What medical reasons could there possibly be for this, the Greek physician does not explain.

In Southern Brazil, a woman makes sure from the start that her first child will be a boy by wearing something blue underneath her wedding dress when she gets married. In parts of the Western world, to announce the birth of a child, parents put a ribbon outside their door, pink for a girl and blue for a boy. Little boys are dressed in blue while pink is the color for girls. In America we say that the bride should wear "something old, something new, something borrowed, and something blue."

In the hills of Appalachia in the Southern United States, it is believed that "more active sex" will produce a boy. Boys are also said to be the result when love is made before midnight while girls are procreated after midnight. In other parts of this same general area of the Southern United States, boys are said to be procreated at night and girls during the morning hours.

If this were true, there would be a lot more boys than girls in the state of Tennessee. According to a survey reported in the morning paper of the capital of Tennessee, while most Americans think of breakfast early in the morning, only 7% consider making love (Rutkoski 1990). One college student from this same part of the country is convinced that "if the man is on top," he will generate a male child.

Blacks in the United States are among the few who consider also the woman's behavior during intercourse. For them, if the woman is more active, the baby will be a boy and if the man is more active, it will be a girl.

The Japanese have a team approach to what, after all, is a team effort. If the couple wants a boy, the husband should eat meat and the wife vegetables. If they want a girl, this diet should be reversed.

For some Californians, food also plays a part in determining the sex of the child. A boy will be born to a woman who eats bananas while eating apples favors the birth of a girl child.

In Mozambique, "the roots of certain plants" are ground into powder which the woman eats in order to increase the likelihood of conceiving a male child. She may continue eating this powder during her first month of pregnancy.

In Florida and Virginia, I was told by a couple of college students from the Southern United States, the phase of the moon at the time of conception determines the sex of the child, but nobody could recall for sure whether boys were conceived under the waxing or the waning moon.

In the Turkish countryside, it is believed that women change their blood every four years. In the fifth year, fresh blood dominates and increases the likelihood of having a female child.

It is known that in the less developed world, there are people who do not see any connection between sexual intercourse and pregnancy. What was new for me was to learn that there is at least one society where people believe that the sex of a child can be influenced at will even after the woman has conceived. On the islands of Sumatra, when a woman is pregnant, her sister-in-law makes an image of a male child and places it before her. To secure male offspring, a woman will also press to her abdomen a fruit resembling the male organ, which she then passes on to a woman who has borne nothing but boys (Frazer 1930, vol. 1, p. 72).

In a similar vein, the Chinese used to believe that during pregnancy a woman can influence the sex of her child by looking intensely at children of the desired sex.

How to detect the sex of the child by looking at the woman who carries it

While relatively little seems to be said on how to assure the production of a male heir, quite a few people are convinced that they can tell if a pregnant woman is carrying a male or female child just from the way she looks. Some of these observations are totally contradictory when one compares one culture with another. So far, none is supported by medical evidence.

In all races, men are taller than women and baby boys weigh more at birth than girls. Northern European babies are heavier than Central and Southern European babies, but the proportion of boys to girls remains the same, according to various standard textbooks for pediatrics. Many people believe that if the woman is very big, she must be carrying a boy. For the same reason, they believe that if she carries the child in the lower part of the abdomen, it must be a boy because his weight pulls him down.

An exception is Somalia, where an expected daughter is said to be heavier than an expected son. Similarly, for the Zuni Indians, girls are said to be larger than boys.

Many people consider the shape of the mother's belly to be indicative of the sex of the child inside. I found the same belief in North America, Central and South America, the Middle East, Africa, and the Far East. If the belly protrudes forward, "like a pencil," as they say in Mozambique, she carries a boy. It's a girl if her belly looks round, or she increases in size especially toward the sides, coming to "look like a watermelon," as described in Brazil. In Iran the folk saying is that if the mother swells and her belly becomes wide and she looks less attractive, she expects a girl. If her stomach is pointed and she becomes more attractive, it's a boy.

Hippocrates believed that the male embryo is carried on the right side while the female is on the left (Hippocrates vol. 4, 1931, Aphorism XLVIII, p. 171). As there is no medical evidence to support this belief, it may be assumed that it is based on the association of strength with maleness. In the human, the right side is usually stronger than the left side.

The Chinese believe that boys move more forcibly than girls inside the womb and thus the intensity of the kicking will tell the mother what to expect. Interestingly, in the United States, gynecologists are convinced that girls move more actively than boys. In Somalia, this idea is extended to the delivery. When the pain is more acute, it predicts the arrival of a son. In Japan, morning sickness is said to be more severe for women expecting a boy.

Many folk beliefs consider hormonal influences. In Taiwan, the male hormones of the fetus are said to make the mother's face break out. In the United States, the inhabitants of Utah hold the opposite opinion (Fife 1976, p. 282). There, a mother's bad complexion is due to a girl in her womb who takes the beauty away from her face. In El Salvador too, a female fetus is said to rob a woman of her beauty. In Turkey, they give no reason, but simply say that a woman becomes prettier when pregnant with a male child and less attractive when she carries a girl. Hippocrates too believed that boys cause a good complexion and girls a bad one (Hippocrates 1923–1988, vol. of 1931, Aphorism X, 41, p. 169). In Brazil, a girl is said to make the mother's facial skin get brownish and boys make her feet swell. If she expects a girl, her eyes look like "goat's eyes."

The Japanese associate the facial expression more with the traditional attitudes of the sexes than with beauty. If her face looks stern or angry, the woman carries a male child. A gentle face indicates that a girl is expected.

In the state of Tennessee in the United States one has to wait until the last trimester of pregnancy to figure out the sex of the expected child. At that time, the male hormones are said to cause hair to grow on the mother's body. A college-educated woman from that state said that she actually experienced this growth, as described in tradition.

In the hills of Kentucky and North Carolina, also in the United States, the inhabitants have a way of divining the sex of the expected child. They string the woman's wedding ring on a cord and dangle it over her abdomen. If the ring swings from side to side in a circular fashion, it will be a girl. It is the general belief that circular movements indicate girls.

In another part of the Southern United States, in the state of Georgia, the people attach a needle on a string and hold it over the woman's head. The direction in which the needle swings indicates the sex of the child. I cannot tell my readers which direction indicates which sex because the young man who told me about this custom remembered his grandmother doing this but could not recall which was which.

In Brazil, too, a needle is attached to a string. If it moves across, it indicates the presence of a male child, if it swings in circles, there is a girl, and if it flops, there will be no child and a miscarriage is expected. I read that the mother's position during sleep varies with the sex of her fetus, but it was not indicated on which side is indicative of which sex (Kruger and Maetzold 1983).

A Kurdish man from Iran told me that there are many folktales on how to foretell the sex of an expected child. He did not remember the details, but he recalled that the child's sex is believed to show from the way the woman eats.

In ancient Egypt a pregnant woman would handle a plant of barley and a plant of wheat. If the barley sprouted first, the child would be a boy; if the wheat sprouted first, it would be a girl (Erman & Krebs 1899, in Kahlo 1930/1933, p. 520). In the middle ages, the Germans performed the same wheat and barley test, but with exactly the opposite interpretation (Boyer 1607, in Kahlo 1930/1933, p. 520; see also Paullini 1714).

In the Amazon state of Brazil, they put the heart of a chicken in a frying pan. If the heart splits open, it will be a girl and if it remains intact, it will be a boy. A middle-class college-educated woman from Brazil actually told my son that some people don't believe in this practice, but that her aunt did it and it worked.

In Turkey, you have to put salt on the woman's head without her knowledge. If she starts scratching the upper side of her body, she expects a girl. If she scratches the lower part, it is a boy. This is sometimes done just for fun when guessing games are played.

In Liberia, they place a baby girl on the pregnant woman's lap. Even if the baby has a strong need to urinate, she will not, knowing that underneath there is another girl. If the pregnant woman is carrying a boy, the baby girl in her lap will always urinate. Conversely, a baby boy will urinate on a girl in the womb.

It is clear that through the ages, couples have tried to find a way to guess the sex of the child they were expecting. This is innocuous enough and many of those who were interviewed indicated that this is done mostly for fun, as there is really nothing they can do, once the sex of the fetus is established.

Today there are medical tests available that will reveal the sex of the unborn child. These tests are performed to rule out birth defects; but sometimes the results of the test are used by parents to abort a child if it is of the "wrong" sex, as I pointed out before.

Conclusion

For a linguist this was one of my most interesting research projects. It shows how closely language and culture relate and how changes in culture affect changes in language and then, in turn, the language reinforces the new cultural norms. One only has to consider the most recent definition of *taikyó* as referring to the expected child, "male or female."

It also shows that most moral concepts are culture-specific. For the groups that kill children right after birth in periods of famine, this procedure seems less cruel than to let the entire tribe starve. It is a form of birth control that would not be considered acceptable in the more developed nations. These developed nations may practice abortion which amounts to the same thing only a little earlier in time. In the United States, it is called "reproductive freedom" by its supporters and "killing" by its detractors. The symbolic power of language is evident in the ever changing terms both parties in the conflict use.

While the chapter on fertility propitiation rites showed the semiotics of power manifest in language as well as in the procreation of children, this chapter showed that the concept of power expressed in the birth of a child has its degrees. More power is conveyed in the birth of a male child than a female. This parallels usage in the Japanese language and even in languages, like English, that have no codified system of men's and women's language. In English, the masculine pronoun "he" is also used as the generic pronoun. The generic "he" nowadays is frequently replaced by "he/she" which parallels the greater acceptance of women in professional positions of power.

I hope my readers found food for thought in this chapter and will not dwell on some of the sadness and cruelty I had to mention within its context.

References

Babylonian Talmud (1965). English translation by Maurice Simon. London: Soncino.

Boyer (1607). *Neuvermehrte heilsame Dreckapotheke.*

Durant, W. (1935). *The story of civilization Part I. Our Oriental heritage.* New York: Simon and Schuster.

Erman, A. & Krebs, F. (1899). *Aus den Papyrus der königlichen Museen.* Berlin: W. Spemann.

Fife, A.E. (1976). Birthmarks and psychic imprinting in Utah folk medicine. in W.D. Hand (Ed.), *U.C.L.A. Conference on American Folk Medicine: A Symposium* (held in 1973). Berkeley, CA: University of California Press.

Frazer, G. (1935). *The golden bough* (3rd ed.). New York: MacMillan.

Hand, W.D. (1980). *Magical medicine: The folklore component of medicine in the folk belief, custom and ritual of the peoples of Europe and America.* Berkeley, CA: University of California Press.

Hippocrates (1923–1988). With an English translation by W.H.S. Jones. London: Heinemann and New York: Putman's Sons.

Kahlo, G. (1930–1933). Elementargedanken in Märchen. In J. Bolte & L. Mackensen (Eds.), *Handwörterbuch des deutschen Märchens* (pp. 519–524). Berlin and Leipzig: Walter de Gruyter.

Kirkwood, R.C. (1990). China's iron-fisted population control (Review of *Slaughter of the innocents* by John Aird). *The Wall Street Journal*, May 14, p. A-14 (The Bookshelf).

Kristoff, N.D. 1990. Some Chinese are warming to one-child limit, (The New York Times News Service). *The Sunday Tennessean*, May 13, p. 3-G.

Kruger, S. & Maetzold, L. (1983). Practices of tradition for pregnancy. *Maternal Child Nursing Journal*, *12*, 135–139.

Leo, J. (1989). Baby boys to order. *U.S. News and World Report*, 106 (January 9), p. 59.

McGowan, J. (1989). In India, they abort females. *Newsweek* CXIII, No. 5, p. 12.

Paullini, C.F. (1714). *Neu-vermehrte heylsame Dreck-Apotheke*. Frankfurt am Mayn: Verlegung Friedrich Knochen und Söhne.

Rutoski, R. (1990). Routines: Ironing wins over sex in the morning. *The Sunday Tennessean*, May 27, p. E-1.

Sorel, N.C. (1989). *Ever since Eve*. New York: Oxford University Press.

Burial Rites for a Miscarried Fetus and Religious Beliefs about the Personhood of the Unborn

Introduction

This is a book about the active life and the individual personality of the little child growing in its mother's womb. It was not written exclusively for pregnant women but it is, of course, of special interest to mothers and fathers expecting a child.

Taikyō counsels pregnant women not to dwell on morbid thoughts. Why, then, should they read about the burial rites of children that die before they are born? Because, it is through some of these burial rites that we truly learn about the love and respect the world's religions attribute to the human being in its earliest stages of life. We also see that the little child in its mother's womb is already considered endowed with personhood. The dignity which is accorded to its final rites is the greatest recognition of the personhood of the fetus.

This, therefore, is not a chapter about death but about life. It was my research on burial rites which, more than any other research in this book, made me aware that in many cultures the child is considered part of its community long before it can physically mingle with its fellow community members. Among the Kurds, Muslim or Christian as they may be, the child is considered a member of the community as soon as it is known that a woman is pregnant. Conception, not birth initiates it into the clan.

All cultures perform the final rites with some religious practices. I will therefore describe the burial customs religion by religion. Of course, there are cultural variations within religions of such broad geographical diffusion as Buddhism and Catholicism. In instances where the parents have converted to a non-ancestral religion, such as from African animism to Western Christianity, the older culture often maintains a strong hold in such vital matters as those relating to bearing a child.

One cannot understand the attitude of different cultures toward the unborn child without looking at the religions practiced by the peoples within each culture. In some cases, differences in religion make for the formation of actual subcultures. In other instances, religion carries much less of an impact. In Japan it is so common to have a Shinto wedding and a Buddhist funeral that some Buddhist temples have begun to post notice that they are also open for weddings.

The world over, codified religions are more recent than the basic folk customs and they certainly have never totally supplanted the latter. When looking at the influence religious beliefs have on pregnant women, one must consider these beliefs jointly with the prevailing folkways. Some women rely more heavily on folk tradition, others more on religion, when the two systems do not coincide. Sometimes, they are aware of the theoretical conflict, and sometimes, they are not or, simply, feel that tradition takes precedence.

Every person also manifests variant degrees of allegiance toward religious prescriptions. A classic example is the obstetrician who wanted to speak in the church of the priest who had attacked him for performing abortions. He felt his request was justified because the majority of his clients were members of precisely that church (Goodman 1989).

The reverse is also true. The religious establishment may turn a blind eye to practices it feels incapable of overcoming. Female infanticide is by no means condoned by Islam; albeit it is a widespread practice in several Muslim countries. The same people who scorn abortion have no qualms about killing little girls. There, the lack of abortions can be explained by the unavoidable possibility that the aborted fetus might be of the male sex (Gatskill, in preparation). What the future will bear, now that the sex of a child can be determined before birth, we do not know.

In addition to these discrepancies between religion and its observance, there are what might be termed religiously pluralistic usages. Young parents who have converted to another religion, more often than not, still feel a profound obligation to observe the rituals of their ancestors and to comply with the wishes of their baby's grandparents. This I have particularly observed among persons from Africa and Asia.

Religion is only one of many factors that influence the attitude people have toward their offspring growing in the womb. What determines their attitudes, like all other aspects of everyday life, is primarily the culture to which they belong.

Culture is a composite of religion, family and family descent, social class, education, political and social status, the physical environment, and even the memory of customs which are no longer observed. It is the sum of all patterns of behavior which are not biologically transmitted. Some forms of culture are taught to the young, but the majority is absorbed through participant observation.

Religions change over time and these changes are generally codified after awhile. Cultures too change, but in a more imperceptible manner. It is much easier to define the boundaries of the various sects which make up each of the major religions than to categorize the subdivisions which constantly form and regroup themselves in each culture.

Mothers also have instinctual behaviors and it is doubtful that cultures can suppress them forever. Classic example are the sterile pregnancy and birthing conditions of middle class America which are gradually giving way to more "old-fashioned," "natural" and gentler customs of bringing a new life into this world.

As said above, families may observe the rituals of the religion of their ancestors in addition to the precepts of their current religion. But, to whatever degree mothers adhere to, or even know, the tenets of their religion, it is essential to know what these are if we wish to find out how different peoples perceive the unborn.

All these variations aside, the most relevant factor in the dating of the personhood of the unborn and the burial customs for a miscarriage or a stillbirth is the religion of the parents. Once it became clear to me that my findings have to be grouped by the various religions, I still had to decide on a logical sequence of my material.

I had several options. One was to go from the major religions to the minor ones. But I excluded this option because of the problem of deciding whether a major religion was so defined by the sheer number of its adherents, by the size of the territory where its adherents lived, or by the spread of these believers across the globe.

A second option which I discarded was to go from the more ancient belief systems to the more recent ones. This did not prove a good idea because the origin of some religions is so remote in time that it is impossible to date their beginnings. A third option was to move along from one part of the globe to the next in geographical progression. Here the problem was to decide where to start. Going from East to West or vice versa was totally arbitrary, but could be interpreted as a conscious choice and lead to unwarranted interpretations.

I concluded that the best sequence was one that was totally arbitrary and did not lend itself to any rationale. The reader will find the material presented in alphabetical order. This sequence has the added advantage that it makes it easy to find what one is interested in if one does not care to read the chapter in its entirety. I do hope, nevertheless, that this chapter will be read in its entirety. I personally found it quite rewarding to see how much more we have in common than what divides us as members of the human race.

It is clear that physiologically, from embryo to fetus to baby, all humans follow the same path. It is equally clear, now that we have a more complete understanding of the intellectual development of the child before birth, that here the same holds true. I have suggested at the meetings of the Language Origins Society since its formation that if we want to study the beginning of language, we have to start with the rudimentary forms of communication between the mother and the child in her womb. A miscarried or an aborted fetus is not a lifeless piece of flesh but a rudimentary human being that has lost its life.

Birth control, abortion and infanticide are problems of vital concern the world over and have been with us from the beginning of history. The military powers of antiquity condemned abortion because of their constant need for soldiers (Durant 1935, p. 275). In Assyria, abortion was a crime punishable by death (Ibid.). In ancient Persia, "fornication, even adultery, might be forgiven, if there was no abortion" and the penalty for the latter was death (Ibid., p. 376). In ancient India, "there was no birth control and abortion was condemned as a crime equal to the murder of a Brahmin" (Durant 1935, p. 489).

Small nations, in need of population increase, have similar concerns, but only in zones where there is adequate food supply. The Hebrew Bible opposes birth control, such as a man "spilling his seed" (Genesis XXXVIII:9). Abortion is never mentioned in the Bible which makes one assume that it was not practiced. The injunction to "be fruitful and multiply" is twice commanded (Genesis I, 2 and Genesis IV, 11). Unmarried men and childless women had low social status and still do so among traditional Jews and Muslims. The different perception among Christians originated in the 4th century, following St. Augustine.

Nomads and small nations living where food is not plentiful tend to favor birth control and abortion. Among the Papuans, abortion is practiced on a large scale.

As an alternative to birth control and abortion, we find infanticide. American newspapers keep reporting about newborn babies left to die in garbage pails, toilet tanks, and along highways.

In antiquity, the Greeks exposed unwanted children to die in the woods. In ancient Arabia, girls were sacrificed to the gods (Durant 1935, p. 291). The custom of the Phoenicians to offer children, especially well-bred boys, to Moloch spread throughout the ancient Middle East to the point that the Hebrew Bible saw the need for a strong injunction against throwing children into ritual fires (Deuteronomy XII, 31).

Miscarriage, stillbirth and abortion

As medical science progresses world-wide, there arise problems in all cultures which the traditional religions have not anticipated. We are entering a highly controversial field which may not be of interest to all of the readers of this book. This entire section can easily be skipped without losing the continuity of the book. I was tempted to exclude this material but, as medicine progresses even further, many readers may wish to know about the potential use — and abuse — of fetal tissue.

As I have shown in a previous chapter, the timing of a child's birth depends largely on when the child is biologically ready to leave the womb. It is the child's brain which coordinates the nervous system governing the relevant muscles inside the mother which must be activated to allow for the child to come out. The common wording is "to be pushed out," but one should not forget that in reality it is for the child to "push itself out." Once the child leaves the comfort of its mother's womb and enters the outside world, it emits a cry of anguish, joy, or just plain self-assertion, depending on how one interprets the first emission from a healthy baby's lungs into the open air.

But what about the child that has been forced out against its volition before its time was ripe? In the earliest stages of gestation it may not yet feel anything. It has no form, is only a blob of blood and flesh. But very soon, at ten weeks of conceptual age, it starts to have rudimentary brain waves. When the fetus is seventeen weeks old, these brain waves become more varied and when it has been in its mother's womb for three months, its brain waves clearly indicate that it could be capable of feeling pain during its expulsion and subsequent death. From that time on, the consciousness of the fetus increases ever more. The period of "quickening" at three months is indeed considered a milestone for the fetus in many cultures.

What about the mother? How does she feel? One might think that if a woman voluntarily kills her fetus by abortion, she might feel only relief and nothing else. Even for prostitutes, for whom getting pregnant is sort of an accident on the job, it is not necessarily so. Some women develop guilt feelings years after an abortion while other women feel relieved and are happy with their decision ever after.

For my survey, a dozen blue and white collar women were asked whether they would feel differently if they had an abortion or a miscarriage, and the majority answered that it would make no difference. One blue collar father said he would feel worse if his wife had an abortion "because she would have caused the loss of the child herself."

Press and television coverage dealing with the loss of life of the unborn child is mostly concerned with the debates about abortion. Miscarriage is largely ignored because it does not lend itself to political discussions. When newspapers report on abortion, they emphasize the gory death of the little fetus or point out the unloved existence the unwanted child would have had if it been allowed to live. They also talk about the psychological implications of a mother's decision to abort or the father's potential right to have a say in such a decision.

Television likes to show pro-choice women marching for freedom from sex discrimination and demanding their civil rights. Other times it shows pro-lifers in a riotous fashion accusing their opponents of being a group of murderers. The media do not generally talk about the feelings of the parents when the abortion of a keenly desired child was necessary to save the mother's life, as in such cases there is no guilt, just immense sadness. It is a sadness comparable to the loss of a child through miscarriage.

Attitudes toward the medical use of fetal tissue

Not much is said or written about what is to be done with the little body that was expelled. This is in sharp contrast to the well-defined regulations for the disposal of a corpse of a person that has lived. People all over the wold know that it would cause grave damage to the living if it were simply left there to decompose. Some communities bury the corpse in the ground or inside a special building. Others cremate the body. In some parts of India it will be put on the rooftops to be devoured by birds of prey so that it will not contaminate the earth.

Psychologists and medical staff do not always believe that a mother should grieve even over a stillbirth. They think that a grieving woman is a "problem mother" and should be sedated. Instead of a dignified burial, the little corpse would be eliminated as fast as possible so there will be nothing to remind the mother of what has happened (Phipps 1981, p. 2).

Some people leave their body to a medical school so that even after death they may be useful to mankind by advancing medical research. Others lovingly donate their organs so that the blind may see, or a child may live through the implant of a liver. Sometimes autopsies have to be performed for the sake of justice in order to establish cause of death.

People who donate their body or their organs make this decision while they are alive. In the case of an autopsy, the coroner has to request a permit from the next of kin. Westerners usually agree, but Orientals weigh the benefits of justice on earth against the peace of the deceased and frequently do not grant permission for an autopsy.

The corpses of children that are miscarried or aborted raise identical problems when the decision is left to their parents. But in many instances the decision of how to dispose of the dead fetus is left to third parties. In cases of forced abortions in the People's Republic of China, seldom do the parents get permission to bury their offspring. This government regulation was loathed by all the Chinese I interviewed. As one father put it, "as if it did not hurt enough to take the child away from us, they do not even let us bury our own flesh and blood."

In voluntary abortions in the United States and Europe there are no such complaints. In "back alley" abortions the mother herself discards her lifeless fetus. Together with full-term babies exposed to die or be killed immediately after birth, such tiny corpses may be found in garbage cans. The term babies are usually buried at city expense, the small fetuses not necessarily so. The police start an investigation for a viable baby, but not for a fetus below viability. This might change as recently murder charges have been pressed for the murder of a fetus by a man who shot the mother and only killed her six-month-old fetus (Loggins 1991).

The medical literature is concerned almost exclusively with stillbirths or perinatal deaths or, at the most, late miscarriages (Kirkley-Best & Kellner 1982; Stringham et al. 1982; Lovell 1983).

In the industrialized world, when a pregnant woman goes to a private obstetrician or to an abortion clinic, she knows that her fetus will be "disposed of" and prefers not to think about it. The little corpses are either discarded like refuse, incinerated, or sold to cosmetic firms which specialize in expensive skin creams. More recently, they are sold to pharmaceutical concerns or utilized for medical research.

It is easy to condemn the use of human fetuses for the benefit of the wrinkle-free face of a wealthy matron, but when it comes to the use of a dead body, be it that of an adult or a little fetus, for the purpose of healing, the answer is far from simple. Recent research into Parkinson's disease has most vividly raised this issue. Fetal tissue also appears to be beneficial for juvenile diabetes, Huntington's disease, and Alzheimer's.

In April 1989, the U. S. Department of Health and Human Services issued an order barring researchers at the National Institutes of Health from performing any experiment involving human fetal tissue. In November 1989, the Department of Health and Human Services extended this ban on all federally funded research involving fetal tissue transplants. For those readers who want to follow the relevant discussion that took place at the U. S. Department of Health and Human Services, I refer to an excellent editorial in the American weekly *The New Republic* (Fetal flow 1990).

Its author asks, quite poignantly; "How exactly does one justify sending fetal tissues to the incinerator when it could be used to save lives?" He then lists plausible objections, the most obvious being that women might undergo abortions for the purpose of selling the fetal tissues. But such fears he considers quite illusory because "the sale of fetuses, like the sale of organs for transplant, is already illegal." Personally, I am not so sure there might not be a black market for fetal tissue and, as such sale does not cause permanent harm to the donor, it might become far more extensive than the already existing black market for organ transplants. The potential for abuse exists in everything. But I would like to ask whether it should override the immense benefits fetal tissue can provide for the sick?

The editorial continues, quoting James O. Mason, assistant to the U. S. Secretary of Health and Human Services, who is worried that a woman might get an abortion for altruistic reasons, "in order to help future generations via medical research." I think that this is highly unlikely. When I mentioned this idea to a young woman, she replied that "whoever thinks that a woman would sacrifice her child, is crazy." In any case, for the time being, the supply of fetal tissue far exceeds the demand.

Paradoxically, it is still permissible in the United States to use fetal tissue for cancer research, but if the research leads to a cure, the healing cells cannot be implanted. The whole area is full of paradoxes. The abortion clinics are not obligated to ask the mother for permission before they give away the fetal tissue. But if a removed appendix is given away for research, the person operated on must provide informed consent. It is legal to conduct a heart transplant but illegal to save a person affected by Parkinson's disease through a transplant of fetal brain cells.

From a humanist, moral perspective, there is no difference between a fetus which is dead because the mother has willed it to be so, a fetus which is dead because the doctor had to make the heartbreaking decision that the life of the unborn was less valuable than the life of a woman whose death would leave her husband a widower and her other children to grow up without their mother, and a fetus which is dead through the natural cause of miscarriage. But if we say that the human body is sacred and has to be buried, we cannot transplant fetal tissue to heal the sick nor use it to find a cure for cancer. By the same reasoning we could not save a life through organ transplants nor dissect a cadaver in medical school. It does not appear reasonable to apply stricter standards to the unborn than we apply to those who were born and lived in the outside world.

On a spiritual, religious level, the entire issue of organ donation, be it from a fetus or from a grown person, is fraught with difficulties. Orientals who believe in reincarnation and/or practice ancestor worship, as well as Jews and Muslims who believe in the resurrection of the dead at the time of Final Judgment, oppose any form of desecration of the human body. These people weigh the benefits of helping the living against the peace of the deceased.

An American physician in a Boston hospital which caters to the local Chinese community told me that he never could get permission to perform an autopsy. The relatives of the dead person fully understood and respected his request but, in terms that were as polite as they were firm, told him that autopsy was out of the question even when it would have been in the interest of justice.

Most Christian religions allow for the medical use of a dead body as well as organ transplants. As far as I know, no authoritative theological consideration has yet been given to the use of fetal tissue.

Burial rites of the fetus according to the world's religions

The problems mentioned above are recent and restricted virtually to the industrialized world. Stillbirth, abortion, and miscarriage are age-old and happen everywhere. To find out about the fate of the embryos and fetuses and even children who were stillborn or lived only a short time, I relied again on the journalistic expertise of my son, Robert Engel. While I read religious tracts, he interviewed leaders of major religions and canvassed people from diverse cultures. We discovered that the attitude of people toward a miscarried embryo or fetus varies greatly depending on a combination of their religion and the society in which they live. But seldom did we find any real consistency within any group concerning what is supposed to be done with the corpse of an unborn child.

Most people that were interviewed for my research were tolerant of the diversity of attitudes. They also admitted their ignorance of other people's belief systems. The same cannot be said of many articles I happened to read in the magazines geared to the American intellectual class which are largely dominated by the feminist movements. One such article categorically asserts that "There are no prayers for the matter of miscarriage, nor do we feel there should be" (Gordon 1990, p. 80). The same author thinks that if a woman wanted to bury a not much formed embryo, "we would have serious concerns about her mental health" (Ibid.). My son's interviews with the ministers of the most diverse religions show an infinitely more charitable approach to a mother's anguish.

As I said before, I will list the religions following the order of the alphabet. The list is far from complete, but it covers a broad enough spectrum of belief systems to give the reader a general idea of how people wish to bury a child that was expelled from the womb before it had a chance to live in the outside world. These burial customs show how much love and respect is due a human being even in its earliest and tiniest stages of growth. The pregnant woman, following *taikyó*, can read about them with great pride in the little one she is carrying, doing everything right so that it will have the best possible chance to grow to term as it should and be born to lead a long, happy life.

I will now present a summary account of how various religions deal with a dead embryo, fetus or stillbirth. I have also included opinions on abortion. On this issue, theologians can be divided into those who believe in absolutes and those who favor situational ethics.

Animatism

Animistic and animatistic religions consider man an integral part of nature and worship the forces of nature and the spirits that inhabit the earth. These belief systems are spread over all the five continents and there is great variation within them.

Here I will report only on the burial rites of the Native Americans. This too really is a very broad definition as each tribe has its own customs and many tribes intermingle Christian beliefs with aboriginal usages. As a general practice, Native Americans bury a miscarriage of any conceptual age in the ground with a simple ceremony and the mother is allowed to grieve. I am also told by Ronald M. Spores, professor of anthropology at Vanderbilt University and a specialist in Mesoamerica, that sometimes, for propitiatory reasons or to appease the ancestors, the little corpse will be left in a cave to be devoured by a wild animal. The dead fetus is always shown great respect.

Bahai

We were informed by the large Bahai Center in Chicago, Illinois, that there will be a simple burial for a dead fetus after five months of gestation. The Bahai families I consulted were of the same opinion, including a Bahai missionary, originally from Iran. The members of the Bahai faith follow the creationist philosophy and believe that a complete soul enters the body at conception.

Buddhism

Buddhism is a proselytizing religion and covers a wide territory. Tibetan and Mongolian Buddhism are heavily influenced by their respective folk religions. Zen Buddhism in Japan has a philosophy of its own. Then there are myriads of sects. What they all have in common is the concept of karma, quite dissimilar from that of the Western concept of soul. Abortion is unacceptable albeit practiced in many parts of the Buddhist world.

I interviewed a Buddhist monk, originally from Burma who is now living in the United States where he received the Ph.D. degree. He was kind enough to come to my home to give me all the time needed to explain his religion and then gave my home a blessing. According to him, the Buddhist practice is that when a baby dies in the womb, there is no religious service, whereas a religious ceremony is essential after a baby is born. Buddhists believe in the recurring cycle of life and death. For a miscarried fetus the group will meditate and send out thoughts of loving kindness so that in his next life the spirit of the unborn will fare better and not die so soon. When a baby has been in his mother's womb for four to five months, it is already a human being and thus can be reborn.

The monk stated that abortion was a secular, not a religious decision. But he added immediately that a Buddhist mother would risk her karma if she chose to abort her fetus. Even if her life were endangered, it would be selfish of her to give more importance to her own well-being than to the child. "A devout Buddhist mother would sacrifice her life for her unborn child."

A Buddhist refugee from Laos and mother of four who has been living in the United States for the past eight years reported that she had actually had a miscarriage, but only after one month of pregnancy. At this stage, she said, "there is not enough life to warrant a burial." Had she lost her baby at seven months, she would have had a burial service.

Another Laotian refugee who has now lived in the United States for six years and who is the mother of one child confirmed basically what the monk had told me. For her there would be a burial ceremony if a fetus died after three months of conceptual age. As such a baby did not succeed in being born, the ceremony would carry his spirit to the next generation.

In addition, two Cambodian refugees were interviewed. One is originally from a rural area; the other from the city. Both men are in their twenties and work in a factory in the United States. Neither of them believes that there would be a burial for a miscarried fetus. A Cambodian refugee woman, however, said that, although she would not have had a burial ceremony for a miscarriage in the United States, she would have had one in Cambodia.

The two Japanese Buddhists I interviewed did not mention re-incarnation. The woman, presently an instructor of Japanese in an American university and the mother of one daughter, said only that in case of miscarriage she would "like to have a burial cere-mony at least." The other Japanese Buddhist was the father of three and a university professor in Japan. He also said that he would like there to be a burial ceremony.

Abortion is legal and widely practiced in Japan even though birth control is considered the better option. In case of abortion, the parents do not want a child right now, but want it to be pos-sible to have this same child in its reincarnation during a sub-sequent pregnancy. To make sure the aborted fetus is not in a state of perfection and thus no longer in need of reincarnation, the par-ents will put a small fish in the dead fetus' mouth. A perfect Budd-hist eats neither meat nor fish. Being presumably in the process of eating fish, their dead child will be reincarnated.

Some Japanese women feel uneasy about having had an abor-tion and will make "an offering at one of the Buddhist temples selling miniature stone statuettes." They will then decorate their statuette with "crocheted hats, plastic bibs, and little toys" (A world conflict on abortion, 1992, p. 23).

All of the mainland Chinese I interviewed defined themselves as atheists, but came from Buddhist families. All wanted to bury a miscarried or aborted fetus in the ground. They would also bring flowers to the gravesite in May during the traditional day of mourning.

Christianity — Catholicism

A Catholic priest does not baptize a stillbirth, but mothers and fathers will do so sometimes by their own decision, my son was told by a Roman Catholic bishop who was most generous of his time. Abortion is forbidden under any circumstances. According to Catholic theology an individual soul enters the embryo right at conception.

Although this belief was shared by all the Catholic persons in-terviewed, burial for a child before it reaches full term does not appear to loom large in their thinking. Even in a country where

Catholicism is the state religion, like Ireland, my son found a grandmother, mother of five, who did not recall what was done with a five-month-old miscarriage of hers. She did remember that her daughter had a stillbirth at term and that baby had "a complete and proper burial."

The Catholic church always had a strong ban on abortion and most recently, has gone as far as excommunicating Catholic doctors who perform abortions. Miscarriage, of course, is a sad accident and obviously not a sin, but as the dead fetus expelled from the womb has a soul and therefore is equally a dead human being, I had expected that Catholic parents would be more concerned about its dignity than devotees of other religions. I really have no explanation of why this was not the case, at least in my small sample. I found as much diversity of opinion among Catholic laymen as I did among other groups. I doubt that these variations in opinion are based on one or the other of the scholastic philosophies about creationism or an evolving soul.

One American father, about sixty years of age, does not believe there would be a burial ceremony at any stage of miscarriage. Another American man, about thirty years of age and the father of seven children, whose wife never had a miscarriage and "certainly never had an abortion" said that he would have a burial ceremony if the fetus were more than six weeks old. Among the female college students I surveyed, two would have no burial at all and two would have one only if the miscarriage occurred during the last trimester.

Among immigrants, opinions vary just as much although all agree that the soul enters the body at conception. A black Cuban woman would have a burial ceremony only after six months of gestation. A woman of the same age, originally from Czechoslovakia would consider burial only for a stillbirth. The opposite was true for a woman from Zaire who had a miscarriage at three months. Her family baptized the fetus and before it was buried they talked with the priest and "prayed for the baby."

Equally, a young woman from the Philippines said that at any period of gestation, the fetus is really a human being and "whatever is left — even if only blood — will be blessed, baptized, and given a proper burial." A black Haitian woman, from a family who used to practice voodoo, said that they have a simple burial for a fetus as little as two months of gestation.

Among Central and South American Catholics, my son talked to a Brazilian couple in their early thirties. They are both professional psychologists and have one child. They were not familiar with what people did in the countryside, but among the educated classes in the cities, they said there will be a funeral for a dead fetus after seven months of gestation. Before that age, the hospital "will take care of it."

A middle class woman from El Salvador said that she was not sure at what stage of gestation the following ceremony will be practiced for a miscarried fetus. She thinks it is after seven months when the little corpse will be put into a box and the father will carry it to the cemetery for burial. She herself lost her first baby after two months of pregnancy and nothing was done for it.

If the life of a woman can only be saved by sacrificing her unborn child, the Catholic religion prescribes that the woman must die, even if she has other children to raise. Few physicians nowadays stick to this injunction and there is debate on this issue within the Catholic laity.

Christianity — Greek Orthodoxy

The Greek Orthodox Church distinguishes between burial rites for children under age seven and burials thereafter. The rationale for this age is not easy to explain because during the burial ceremony for an infant there is no prayer for forgiveness of sins, but such a prayer is said for a child under seven years of age. Age seven is thus not the watershed for accountability for one's sins.

The emphasis in the burial rites for a miscarriage, a stillbirth or a baby is for the mother who needs "healing for her suffering" (Constantinides 1989, p. 15). A much used prayer book has a special section with "Prayers for a woman who has had a miscarriage" (Ibid.). According to the Greek Orthodox parish priest I consulted, the status of the child before birth has not been given much scholarly attention. While the burial of an infant is obligatory, the religious burial of a fetus is optional, depending on the wishes of the mother in cooperation with the priest. The burial ceremony is always an abbreviated one and not like the elaborate funerary rites for an adult.

During a delivery when the emerging child is likely to be a still-birth it is given an "emergency baptism" with just one drop of water and if water is not feasible, it will have an "air baptism." If a stillbirth is recognized only after its death, there will be no baptism. In the case of a miscarriage, it is permissible to baptize the emerging fetus, should the mother so desire, but a dead fetus cannot be baptized. Abortion is not allowed.

Christianity — Protestantism

Protestantism has many denominations and there is great varia-tion concerning the perception of the unborn. The more liberal denominations are pronouncedly pro-choice while the fundamen-talists oppose abortion. The burial of a fetus has not received great attention and opinions differ even within the same denomination. For the purpose of this book, ministers as well as laymen were interviewed.

Christians

Three mainstream American women, all mothers, who defined their religion as Christian, said that they did not know how to answer a question on whether a miscarriage should have a burial because they had never thought about it. An unmarried, young Christian woman suggested a burial ceremony might be appropri-ate if the miscarriage occurred after the third month.

Independent Christians

A forty-year-old native of Brooklyn, New York, who now lives with her Southern husband in a commune in Tennessee and clas-sifies her religion as Independent Christian said that she herself never had a miscarriage, but a friend of hers, "whose baby died in the womb" during the third trimester of her pregnancy, had a burial ceremony for it. They had no minister present, but the burial was conducted with a religious ceremony of her own de-sign.

Three female American undergraduate students also defined their religion simply as Christian. One would have no burial at any stage of pregnancy, the other one would have a burial at any stage, and the third one would have a burial after six months.

A Korean Christian, mother of three, who has lived in the United States for eighteen years, would not even have a burial service for a stillbirth. One mother of a baby, a Christian from mainland China who grew up in Singapore and now lives in the United States, wants a burial service for a fetus after the third month of gestation.

Amish (The Old Order Mennonites)

An Amish couple from northern Indiana told my son when he was in Indianapolis that they would "bury what's there," but have a religious ceremony only after six months of gestation.

To the Amish elder the question of when the soul enters the fetus was irrelevant because the commandment "Thou shalt not kill" is the one essential consideration and there is no need to dwell on theoretical consideration. He equated abortion with murder. "What is done is done," he said, and we have to take the consequences.

Baptists

I interviewed three Baptists. A 35-year-old Black father of four from Savannah, Georgia, said that he believes that the embryo has a soul immediately after conception, but that he had not thought about possible burial for a miscarriage. A black undergraduate university student in Nashville, Tennessee, originally from Nigeria, was still single, had thought about it and advocated burial after the first trimester. A white factory worker, in his late thirties and father of three, would consider a burial service only for a fully developed baby.

Free Will Baptists

A Free Will Baptist, chairman of the theology department of one of their colleges, said that he did not recall ever going to such a funeral, but was sure a fetus would get the same treatment as a stillbirth. Before saying so, he remarked that a miscarriage must be much more devastating for the woman than most people think. Frankly, I wondered why more people had not mentioned the pain a mother must experience before they would start talking about how a fetus was to be buried. It is possible that they did not talk about matters of feelings because the vast majority of our interviews were conducted by my son, a male journalist in his late twenties. But then, the few people interviewed by women did not delve into sentiment either.

Most Free Will Baptists believe that the soul enters the body at conception, but there is no official stand on this issue. The Free Will Baptist theologian said his church had no clear cut guidelines on abortion as the Roman Catholic Church does. Abortion as a means of birth control is wrong, but if a mother's life were jeopardized, he would choose to save the mother's life over the life of the unborn child.

Southern Baptists

Two undergraduate males were Southern Baptists. One, from Texas, would have a burial only after a full-term birth. The other one, from Georgia, would have a burial if the fetus died during the last trimester of gestation. The soul enters the body at conception, said a woman from Tennessee, and she could have a burial at whatever stage of gestation.

Christian Fundamentalists

A Christian Fundamentalist black woman from Liberia, married to a white American man and living in the Southeastern part of the United States said that she was quite familiar with the African customs of her country of origin. In case of miscarriage, during the early months of gestation there will be no burial, but once the fetus is formed, it will receive a burial, albeit a very simple one. Her family in Liberia is Christian.

Church of Christ

Among the members of the Church of Christ, I separately interviewed a husband and wife, both from the Southern United States, in their late thirties and the parents of four children. The husband was not sure because a miscarriage had never happened either to him (he said "to me") nor to his wife. But he probably would have a burial after the first trimester, with only the immediate family present. His wife was less hesitant, but gave basically the same answer, suggesting that after the first trimester there should be a private, non-religious burial with only the immediate family present.

Disciples of Christ

A twenty-five-year-old single man from Georgia who had graduated from a prestigious university and was working in a bookstore was a member of the Disciples of Christ. He suggested there be a burial "when the stage of pregnancy was developed enough that the woman had knowledge of her pregnancy." A male undergraduate student of the same religion held a different opinion. At no stage of gestation would he have a burial for a dead fetus.

Episcopalians

The nine Episcopalians we interviewed held equally divergent opinions. One male executive, age sixty and father of two, considered burial appropriate only for a full-term child. One female undergraduate student considered it appropriate at any stage of conceptual age. Another female undergraduate said exactly the opposite. She wanted no burial at any stage. Four undergraduate women favored burial during the later stages of gestation and one would leave the decision to the parents. The soul is believed to enter the body at conception.

Evangelical Christians

An "Evangelical non-denomination Christian" father of two, in his thirties, advocated a burial for a miscarriage "late in the term." A woman of the same religion and equally mainstream American agrees with him. This mother of one, expecting her second child, would have a burial ceremony "only in the later stages."

Lutherans

The most unexpected answer came from a Zulu woman from South Africa. She is a Lutheran and mother of three, and had experienced both a miscarriage and an abortion. On both of these occasions, she had felt the same grief. For a fetus she would have a burial after six months, when it would be possible to "see whether it was a baby boy." Another Lutheran interviewee, a mainstream American university student, is unsure about what she would decide for a dead fetus.

Methodists

A Methodist minister was contacted by my then assistant Ms. S. Reynolds. As Ms. Reynolds knew this minister personally, she was able to spend much time with him and I appreciate her time as well as his. When asked when he believed the soul enters the fetus, he replied that he did not know when, if it does, at all. After reflecting for a brief few moments, he went on to say that human life begins when there is brain activity in the fetus which he thinks is at about three months of gestation. He feels that human life in a fetus is a slow evolutionary process in the mother's womb. We must make decisions about when there is life based on degrees of life in fetal development. He "had never buried a fetus and this is all he could say in all honesty." Although this minister's answer about the developing soul greatly puzzled my assistant, it did not surprise me because it represents a classic scholastic medieval concept of the soul which is thought of as developing with the body. First there is a vegetative soul, then an animalistic soul, and finally a human soul.

Because he has spent almost thirty years working and living out his ministry in poverty areas of large metropolitan centers, this Methodist minister sees abortion as a distinctive class issue. He never has advised abortion as a solution to a poor, black mother married or single, but he "has seen a lot of traffic on this issue." He will not pass judgment about abortion, although he has never seen any woman go through an abortion who did not have great difficulties afterward. Nevertheless, he would not begin to think of passing a law that took away the decision from the individual

woman. He pointed out that some of the most militant anti-abortionists take very little, if any, stand on issues relating to health
care for the poor or quality of life for this large segment of our
society. However, he joins the anti-abortionists in regretting anything that drifts toward casualness in regard to abortion. He is
equally opposed to the absolute intolerance of the pro-life movement toward anyone who chooses an abortion. From what he has
seen, men and women who have grappled with the question of
abortion do agonize over their decision. When abortion is chosen,
there have always been long-term questions and emotional
struggles months and even years after the abortion. His experience
seems to confirm what pro-life groups assert, that the mother who
aborts never recovers psychologically (Brokaw 1989), but he
added that people must make this agonizing decision in the direction of the situation that will invest them with the most life-giving
force.

He then shared an experience of a woman who lived in public
housing. She was married, tried to use the pill but had serious
complications, so switched to another form of contraception. She
became pregnant. She had not been careless, he said, but had tried
to plan her family. Since she was enrolled in nursing school and
had to finish to get her degree, she finally chose to have an abortion. She was luckier than most women in public housing, he said,
because she had good friends who helped her raise the $350.00
necessary for the abortion, while most women in such conditions
have to resort to dangerous improvisations. Now, he reports, this
woman has finished her nursing school training and has a nice job
in a large hospital. She is pregnant again and happy. Women, he
believes, often must choose what will be most life-giving for those
who already live. For this minister there are no absolutes on the
question of abortion.

As Nashville, Tennessee, where I live, has such a large Methodist population, I was able to contact many members of that denomination.

A Methodist secretary working in the office of a large manufacturing plant, some forty years old and the mother of two,
would give a burial to a miscarried fetus after three months of gestation. Another Methodist, a seventy-year-old man, holding an
executive position in a large company, does not believe in burial
for any miscarriage. Among five female undergraduate university

students, two agreed with this in not having any burials and the other three had never thought about it. Another Methodist, an upper middle class housewife, said that she has had a miscarriage at three months of pregnancy and "there was no burial." She added that "if a premature baby had died, I am not sure what I would have done." The last of the Methodists I interviewed, a graduate student, single and female, found burial feasible only for a stillbirth.

Mormons (Church of Jesus Christ of the Latter-Day Saints)

Two Mormon elders from Utah told me that after three months of gestation, there would be a simple graveside service for a miscarried fetus. The service would be just for family and close friends. A complete religious ceremony would be conducted only for a full-term baby. Abortion is not permitted under any circumstances.

A Mormon, originally from Taiwan, and now living in California, twenty-years old and the father of a four-month-old baby, specified that the simple burial mentioned by the two elders would be held only after five months of gestation.

Pentecostals

Similarly, a twenty-five-year-old Black American mother of two, a Pentecostalist, would not have any sort of burial for a miscarriage.

Presbyterians

Among Presbyterians, three female undergraduate university students were equally divided on the issue. One had not yet thought about the topic, one opted for a burial at five months of gestation, and one considered that the time for the burial would come "when the fetus resembles a baby." A Presbyterian minister told me he could not answer my question about when the soul entered the body. It is an extremely controversial field. Depending on the answer, the church is divided in anti-abortionists and those that allow for abortion before the fetus is viable.

Protestants

Among the people I approached, four adults and four under-graduate students classified their religion simply as Protestant without mentioning a specific denomination. Among the adults, a manufacturing executive from Indiana in his late fifties and father of two, stated that "Any child would have a burial cere-mony, at any stage of death." The other man, a factory worker form Ohio, thirty years of age and the father of four, thought that a burial ceremony becomes due "when the human form is visible." The third adult Protestant was a native of Germany who had come to the United States about thirty years ago. This father of four, who has a middle management position, believes that there should be a burial for a miscarriage after seven months of gestation.

The fourth Protestant was an upper class woman from Brazil, currently in the United States where her husband does research. She said that in the large cities of her country a miscarried fetus will have a regular funeral when the family has control over the matter, but there will never be music, as she had heard "they are doing here." She was not sure how the disposal of the dead fetus was handled when the mother is in the hospital. She was equally unfamiliar with customs in the rural areas.

I also interviewed four undergraduate women. Of these, one would have a burial at any stage of gestation, another only after six months, and two would leave the decision to the parents.

Quakers

We interviewed one Quaker, a female undergraduate student. She would have no burial at any stage for a dead fetus.

Seventh-Day Adventists

Among Seventh-Day Adventists, opinions vary. An upper class black Cuban woman believes that a fetus should have a burial after six months of gestation. A somewhat older Caucasian wom-an from Lima, Peru, who has lived in the United States over twenty years would have a burial earlier, at four months, "when the mother would know that the baby is formed."

A Seventh-Day Adventist Spanish woman from Chile, living in the United States for the past eight years, informed us that only a stillborn would have a burial ceremony. Miscarriages at any age would simply be "discarded."

Christianity — Unitarians

The only Christian denomination with a clearly defined philosophy are the Unitarians. The Unitarian minister and a lay person my son consulted told him that in their group everyone takes responsibility for whatever they do and makes up his own mind, including any practices connected with miscarriage and abortion. This freedom of opinion includes their ministers. One Unitarian minister actively campaigned in the pro-choice movement (Wissner 1989).

Hinduism

Hinduism has several branches, some as separate as Jainism. All agree in the belief in reincarnation. Given that it is a very old religion and practiced over a wide territory, it is not surprising that one encounters much diversity in the treatment of a dead fetus. My son interviewed a Hindu priest, originally from Kannada, India, and currently residing in the United States. He told us that "after the fetus starts to form, there will be a religious burial in the case of miscarriage." A strikingly conflicting answer came from the wife of a Hindu neonatal physician, now at an American research university. Both came from India to the United States some fifteen years ago. This mother of two said that there would not be a service even if a child were to die at three days of life. A young infant or a newborn is not cremated. It is buried in the ground because cremation is a purification ceremony. Without life and sin there is no need for purification. To be cremated the child must be at least two years old.

A physician from Bombay was not of this opinion and said that a very small fetus would only be buried, but a family could wish to cremate a premature baby. Such a family decision is made by its senior members, not just the parents. A thirty-four-year-old mother of two from Northern India who works as a researcher in the United States, would simply "discard" a dead fetus or a still-birth, even at nine months of gestation.

According to Hinduism if a choice has to be made between saving the life of the mother or that of the child, it is the child that has to be saved. Abortion is never an option. The Hindu priest said that if will power were practiced there would be no need for abortions. Intercourse, he further stated, is to be practiced for pro-creation, not just happiness. He then added that one enjoys sex more after a period of abstinence. After all, he mused, this is what Ghandi did.

Judaism

Judaism is a very old religion which is practiced in many parts of Asia, Europe and the Americas. It has many branches, but here I will limit this survey to the three most well-known branches. Em-phasis throughout is on justice and correct behavior and not much on epistemology. In the Torah, the five books of Moses which con-stitute the code of the Jewish religion, there is no mention of soul. Some Jews believe in immortality, some have no opinion, and some believe in reincarnation. One Reform rabbi was inclined to believe that the soul enters the unborn after forty days of gesta-tion, but he commented that "ensoulment" is not a serious issue in Judaism.

All agree that if the mother's life is severely endangered, abor-tion becomes mandatory. The reason for this is given by the me-dieval scholar Maimonides (Yale Judaica Series, vol. 9, p. 196) who states that if the fetus is causing a woman bodily harm, it is equated to a pursuer and potential murderer. According to Jewish law, a bystander is not allowed to remain passive and must assist the pursued, even if it means killing the pursuer. But once the child has emerged, even only partially, it is considered equally a full life like its mother. For a comprehensive treatment of the fetus accord-ing to Jewish law, I refer to an article by rabbi Riskin (1991).

Where there is disagreement is on how much personhood can be attributed to the fetus. In Exodus (XXI, 22) it is written that if a woman miscarries because she is accidentally injured by two men fighting among each other, the man who caused the loss of the fetus shall be fined and "he shall pay as the judges determine."

But if the woman herself is killed, her murderer incurs the death penalty.

Official funerary rites with the recital of the traditional prayer for the dead are obligatory only after a child has lived outside the womb for at least thirty days. But there is nothing to forbid a rabbi to go through mourning rituals in the burial of a stillbirth, a miscarriage, or an abortion. This is considered therapeutic for the parents. On this all branches of Judaism agree.

Conservative Judaism

The conservative rabbi to whom my son spoke always buries the fetus and lets the parents recite any prayers they wish. A Jewish father of three, a professional man in his sixties, had never thought about this and had no answer. A university professor in Israel, in his late forties and the father of four children, also was not aware of the problem, but suggested there be a burial ceremony for a miscarriage during the last trimester.

Orthodox Judaism

The Orthodox rabbi said he would always bury a dead fetus if it had recognizable organs and was beyond the embryonic stage, but he would not have a religious ceremony unless the mother expressed a wish for one. He once was given a little box at a hospital which he took to the cemetery where he quietly buried it. Some Orthodox parents have a male fetus circumcised, but in a very simple operation performed at the gravesite and not the elaborate ceremony that accompanies the circumcision of a live boy.

Reform Judaism

The Reform rabbi would allow for abortion in case of rape, incest, or adultery, or when the woman's well-being is at stake, but always only in the early stages of pregnancy. The Reform rabbis are broader in defining what constitutes a woman's health and include her emotional state. The rabbi said it is a very murky area and he would try to dissuade a woman, but not stand in her way. Whether the fetus is to be buried or not is entirely left to the woman's decision.

Three Jewish female undergraduate students considered a burial for a dead fetus "once it takes a human appearance," at six months of gestation, or only at birth.

Mohammedanism (Islam)

Mohammedanism has many branches, but the fundamental interpretation of the Koran is not very dissimilar. For the purposes of this book I was only able to contact Sunni Muslims. They are not unanimous about what to do with a dead fetus. The leader of a Muslim congregation is called imam. At the suggestion of a Muslim university professor, originally from Iran, my son approached the Sunni imam of Nashville, Tennessee, who is a black man who had converted from Christianity and is said to be very knowledgeable about the religion of Mohammed. This imam told him that there will be a simple burial, without any ceremony. He did not indicate at what period of gestation, but said that according to his religion, the soul enters the body at six months of conceptual age. Mothers are encouraged to be stoic: "If a woman loses three of her children before puberty, she is guaranteed paradise if she is patient and does not lament the death of her children for years." Muslim laymen seemed to believe that the soul enters the body at conception but were unsure about it.

A physician who had left Iran at the time of the Khomeini revolution to live in the United States said that if a miscarriage occurs after the fifth month of gestation there would be a burial, but no religious ceremony. An upper class Iranian mother of three, who came to the United States at the same time, told me that the burial without religious ceremony would be held only after seven months of gestation.

A middle-class refugee from Afghanistan and mother of five was of a very different opinion. According to her, a baby would have to have breathed at least for one second before a burial could take place. If a baby were stillborn, it would not have any funeral service. I failed to ask her whether there could be a burial without a religious ceremony. Another woman from Afghanistan, however, was more in agreement with the Iranian Muslims. She said that "when a baby dies before birth, we take out the baby and bury it like a big person. After three months of gestation it is a real baby, it can move and breathe."

A Muslim woman from Jakarta, now living in the United States and mother of a toddler, said that she would have a burial ceremony if she had a miscarriage after three months of pregnancy.

My son visited with six professional couples originally from Turkey. All were Muslim. Some of them were religious and some were non-observant. In the information they gave there was really no difference. We also interviewed a Turkish couple who were Jews. Their answers did not differ from those of their Muslim fellow-Turks.

Turkey has a secular government which allows abortion and people in the cities take advantage of it. In rural areas, people tend to obey the Koran where abortion is strictly forbidden as a way out of an unwanted pregnancy. In case of miscarriage, city hospitals take care of the dead fetus "in a special way" while in the countryside the fetus is buried with the prayers of the parents and a religious ceremony, except for a miscarriage during the earliest period where there is no recognizable form.

The Koran does not mention abortion, but I am told by all my Muslim friends that it is strictly forbidden in Islam. But I was also told by an observant Muslim woman from Iran that it is sometimes practiced to save the family honor. In such cases, everything is done in great secrecy and thus there is no question of burial for the aborted fetus or embryo.

The Kurdish Muslims allow for abortion to save the mother's life. They bury a miscarriage but the Kurdish man interviewed did not know about the aborted fetus.

Shintoism

For Shintoism, each soul is created at the moment of conception. It survives the death of the body and goes to paradise, immediately or after a period of purgatory. Thus all ancestors are in a spiritual existence and can be worshipped. I did not find any mention of miscarriage or abortion.

No religion

Some persons we approached defined themselves as having "no religion." As this is a very specific statement, I have grouped them here together. Some of the people classified as having no religion called themselves "agnostics" or "atheists." I made no distinction among these three designations

When people indicated that they were members of a certain denomination but not particularly observant, I have still grouped them together with the observant members of their religious affiliation. I have done this because from my long research experience with disparate groups, I came to see that much of what concerns pregnancy and childbirth is tied to tradition.

Among this group was a mainstream American university professor in her late forties and the mother of two. She said she did not know what she would do with a miscarried fetus, but was certain that during the first trimester of pregnancy she would not think of a burial. Another American woman, a professional librarian and mother of three, in her early sixties would have a simple burial for a dead fetus after six months of gestation. An American factory worker, father of two, in his mid-thirties, would have a burial when "the unborn fetus had most of its human features, five months and beyond."

Of five American undergraduate university students, the two males had not thought about this topic. Of the two females, one said it should depend on what the parents wished to do while the other one opted for cremation of the dead at any age, unborn to adult. The third one would have a burial only for a full-term baby.

A recent immigrant from Russia said that in Russia a miscarried fetus "is done away" in the hospital. For a fully developed stillborn, however, there can be a burial if the parents want one.

A Japanese professional and the father of two, who considers himself, like many Japanese do, as observing no religion, told me that for a miscarriage there would be no burial. Once a child is born and registered with the government, if it dies, by law, it must be buried. Some temples and shrines will also bury a miscarried fetus if the parents so desire. In that case, there will not be an official ceremony and "the mother just prays." A Japanese professor in a prestigious university in Japan, father of three, in his late forties, suggested a burial ceremony after six months of gestation.

An immigrant from South Korea who now works in an American factory and who is the father of three adult children said that he really had no ready answer to my question.

All of the mainland Chinese I contacted defined themselves as atheists, but I do not know whether they say so because this is their official status and they might be Buddhists at heart. One Chinese woman, currently in the United States with her husband, a medical researcher, said that a miscarried baby will be buried in the ground and the parents will visit the grave and bring flowers every year at the traditional mourning day in May.

Another Chinese mother of one immediately thought of a forced abortion and answered with the following words: "just a burial. Medically, the operation will be easy if the miscarry [sic] is done early. Spiritually, both the father and the mother would like the burial to be solemn, because this is their flesh and blood. It is not a religious ceremony, but it is a very sad burial."

The three Chinese fathers I contacted seemed to share her opinion. One said, "Miscarry [sic] is terrible and should be avoided if it can. If it were to happen, we don't very often have a burial ceremony. That is to say, it is not complete yet. Usually the hospital will be responsible for this. And sometimes it should be done as early as possible, because the earlier, the mother will be less dangerous during the operation, and less miserable the parents will be." The second man said "if a baby is developed fully, no parents will permit the baby to leave them ... " There is usually a burial, but no religious ceremony. The third man made a distinction between planned and unplanned pregnancies in relation to the status of the fetus which was forced to be expelled.

Conclusion

There are many more religions and it was impossible to cover them all. I tried to have fairly authoritative coverage for all religions mentioned in the book. Time did not permit me to obtain my goals for each religion. The book wants to be an incentive for further study and I hope colleagues will pick up one or the other of the topics covered and explore it to the fullest.

This book does not aim at a comprehensive coverage. It intends to give the reader a broad perspective of how the unborn child is viewed the world over. This chapter has shown that even in death the fetus is treated with respect. I hope that I have given some idea of how members of the major world religions think about the ultimate fate of the little corpse of a child who died before it had a chance to live. It may be buried, cremated, or simply "disposed of by the hospital." Nobody I talked to specified what "disposed of" actually meant and nobody seemed aware of the possibilities of donating parts of the dead fetus for the benefit of the living now or in the future. In general, people had not given much thought to the fate of their dead fetus. An exception were the Chinese who appeared pained at the thought that they were not always allowed to provide a dignified funeral to what they called "their flesh and blood."

The lack of a strong concern for the fate of a fetal corpse is in marked contrast with the fact that parents the world over will pressure their governments to request former enemies to release the bodies of their sons killed in action. Public opinion strongly supports the request for the bodies of fallen soldiers and expects dignified ceremonies for their remains. Soldiers are complete human beings. A fetus is yet incomplete, but it is more than only a potential human being. I hope that my book has shown this.

References

A world conflict over abortion (1992). *World Press Review* October, pp. 22–24.

Brokaw, Tom (Anchor) (1989). *NBC Nightly News*, Jan. 9, Video tape available at the Vanderbilt University Television News Archives.

Constantinides, E. (1989). *The priest's service book* (original Greek text and English translation). Merriville, IN: Fr. Evagoros Constantinides.

Fetal flow (1990). *The New Republic*, 202, No. 1, Issue 3, 9111 (January 1), pp. 7–8.

Gaskill, T. (in preparation). *Ibn Sina's Ontology*. Ph. D. dissertation in progress. Nashville, Tennessee: Vanderbilt University, Department of Philosophy.

Goodman, J. (1989). Doctor wants own say at Mass after priest in abortion protest. *The Tennessean*, January 12, p. 114.

Gordon, M. (1990). A moral choice. *The Atlantic Monthly 265*, issue 4 (April), pp. 78, 80–84.

Kirkley-Best, E. & Kellner, K.R. (1982). The forgotten grief: A review of the psychology of stillbirth. *American Journal of Orthopsychiatry, 52*, 420–428.

Loggins, K. (1991). Charge of murdering fetus city's first. *The Nashville Tennessean*, p. 6-B

Lovell, A. (1983). Some questions of identity: Late miscarriage, stillbirth and perinatal loss. *Social Science and Medicine, 17*, 755–761.

Phipps, S. (1981). Mourning response and intervention in stillbirth: An alternative genetic counseling approach. *Social Biology, 28*, No. 1–2 (Spring/Summer), 1–13.

Riskin, S. (1991). The fetus as potential killer. *Jerusalem Post International Edition*, February 9, p. 23.

Stringham, J.G., Riley, J.H. & Ross, A. (1982). Silent birth: mourning a stillborn baby. *Social Work, 27*, 322–327.

Wissner, S. (1989). Minister calls men to defend abortion rights. *The Tennessean*, Jan. 30, p. 2B.

Yale Judaica Series (1954). *Vol. 9: The code of Maimonides. Book II, The book of torts, laws of murderers*. New Haven, Connecticut: Yale University Press.

Our Individual Personality Is Formed Before Birth

Introduction

As I said in the introductory chapter, I worked over a period of thirty years gathering the material for this book. Over time, I presented my findings at the annual meetings of learned societies. It was quite interesting and rewarding indeed, to see how my subject matter, which at first was considered somewhat irrelevant or odd, gradually gained acceptance and eventually my lectures were eagerly sought after.

I experienced true pleasure in writing each chapter for this book, but the research for this particular chapter is the one that gave me the greatest satisfaction. It enabled me to prove most forcefully that birth is an important event, but it does not represent a radical break between before and after. Life from conception to death is a continuum. From fertilized egg to embryo to fetus to baby to infant to adult, the human being develops physically and mentally according to the interaction between its genes and its environment.

During its prenatal period much more is known about the physical development of the child than about its mental development. This book is concerned primarily with the mental growth of the fetus. If "babies are born ready for social functions" (Chamberlain

1988, p. 81), this readiness must have developed before they were born. Indeed, "even in the womb, babies react differently" (Ibid., p. 53).

The hypothesis

What I want to bring out here is that the unborn already has its own little personality and that this personality will continue throughout life. Individual differences manifest themselves during the intra-uterine existence and not only later in childhood. That the unborn has a distinct personality of its own is not a new discovery, albeit one that is not widely known. It was first asserted by Sir William Liley in 1972 and is more extensively documented by Chamberlain (1988, chapter 4, p. 53–66).

What is new in the research project that will be described in this chapter is the continuity of each child's individual personality between the prenatal and the postnatal period of life. I have asserted this in lectures of mine and the psychologist David Chamberlain (1988) has written about this. The research described in this chapter is the first to empirically document the continuation of this individual personality from before birth to after birth.

To prove this I conducted a survey among women who had borne more than one child. This chapter will present the results of my survey. It was a fairly simple survey, but one that proved unexpectedly very time-consuming.

Research design

I had two options to design my research. One was the so-called scientific method which stipulates an organized body of knowledge built on objective experiments. I would have had to expose a number of pregnant women to ultra-sound testing at regular intervals. Then, after their birth, the babies would have to be videotaped at regular intervals. Some years later, when these same women would be pregnant again (and hopefully still living in the same city where I live) the same procedures would be applied. Within some five years or so, the two sets of findings could be compared with the help of the computer.

I never really contemplated to use this "exact" methodology. That it is expensive and cumbersome is a minor stroke against it. My major objection to such a design is that it violates the naturalness condition. Like so many tests performed in psychology and other social sciences it looks good on paper, but given the artificial circumstances, it is not fully reliable.

I prefer to collect "anecdotal evidence" to practicing pseudoscience. My subjects were a convenience sample over a six-month period. It, frankly, was as random as can be. I started out asking a woman whether she had noticed differences in the behavior among her children, making sure, as much as possible, that I would not present loaded questions.

I had designed a simple and brief questionnaire (see appendix) and had not anticipated that some interviews would last for over two hours. The purpose of my research was to find out whether there is a similarity in the behavior of the child in the womb and later in the world outside. To ask the pertinent questions, I needed women who had borne at least two children. It was not difficult to find these women but the problem was to stop them from talking. As they did me a favor, neither my assistant, Ms. Yoshiko McCollough, nor I wanted to be impolite.

The interview started out by asking these mothers about any differences they might have noticed in the behavior of their children when they were little. "Oh yes," virtually every woman said, and then they proceeded telling me at length how gifted and successful their children were. The baby that was the quiet type is now a renowned medical researcher. The answer was accompanied by details about the universities her son or daughter had attended, scholarships won, prominent friends acquired, not to mention the equally intelligent spouse. The other child was the lively one and is now in the process of building a successful business career involving extensive travel. Mothers love to talk about their children's successes.

Being a polite person, I could not possibly interrupt these proud moms. Eventually, sometimes even without need for prodding on my part, they came to tell about how their children when they

were toddlers already showed the signs of their different orienta-
tions, the quiet child liked to sit and watch television or be read
to while the lively one used to run around, jump up and down on
the furniture, and "keep the parents really busy." Being told about
the children's development in reverse order puzzled me until I understood why this was so and what implications it has to a
mother's attention to prenatal care.

I guess my readers will sympathize with how I felt spending
hours on end, entire days, to listen to reports that seemed totally
useless for my research. But, really, I have never undertaken any
empirical research project that did not reveal something new to
me, beyond my original design. These irrelevant data combined
with the useful data on which I will report below showed that
what mothers do for their children is geared to ready them for the
real world. Playing with a toddler is not an end in itself. We know
that children learn through playing. Much of the parental activity
is instinctual and the child's learning process comes about largely
by osmosis.

Eventually, I asked the mother whether she recalled her children's behavior while she was carrying them. If I got a blank stare,
I had no choice but to tell her that I wanted to know whether the
rambunctious, lively toddler was more active, kicking harder, and
moving around more while in the womb, and whether the more
quiet child was already more quiet during the prenatal stage of
life. I tried my best to keep a nonchalant tone of voice, leaving
open the impression that I might possibly doubt this.

As I said in the beginning of the chapter, my objective was to
test my hypothesis that the child's personality is formed before
birth. If I am correct, there will be a continuity of behavioral patterns from the prenatal to the postnatal period of the child's life.

The data

The answers can be divided into three groupings. Among American women, by far the largest number told me that they did not
recall the behavior of their children before birth. All they did is
watch for continued movement in the womb because this is the

sign that everything is fine and proceeding normally. Several women who had borne more than four children looked at me and with a condescending smile told me that I had only two children while they had four, (or five, or six, as the case may be) and were "just plain too busy caring for them to pay attention to anything."

Other women had only two or three children, but had them "so long ago" that they could not possibly remember such details. Among the younger women, some said they did not pay attention to the movements in their womb once quickening had occurred and they were certain that the child was alive and well. They simply did not believe in current fads of talking to an unborn child. Besides, even if they did, they were too busy doing housework and keeping their job to be bothered with anything.

Among the Japanese women, a limited number of the older ones did not recall fetal movements but said that if they were pregnant today, they certainly would pay attention. The Japanese women, like their American counterparts, tended to gloat in the achievements of their offspring. Of whatever nationality, all of the women contacted, I am pleased to say, considered it plausible that its fetal behavior corresponds to the personality a child will show later on. Needless to say, any conversation eliciting such comments happened only after I had finished the formal interviewing process. Formal is really not the right word. All interviewing was done in a casual style. It simply means that I discontinued taking notes on my little elegant (i. e., non-intimidating), non-professional note pad.

Many of the mothers I interviewed over the years have told me that they sing when they are working around the house, and that they sang more when they were pregnant. The majority of the American women did not sing on purpose to soothe their fetus. They sing for their own pleasure, they said.

Some younger American women and virtually all of the younger Japanese women caressed their pregnant abdomen and spoke to the expected child. The Japanese mothers read aloud from books and played music. Their admitted purpose was not so much to soothe their unborn child, but to expose it to intellectual activities as early as possible to make it easier for the child to excel later on. *Taikyó* is conscious behavior.

It was interesting to notice that all of the women who had been actively involved with the children they were carrying remembered distinctly how these unborn children behaved. There were, nevertheless, several women who did not practice *taikyó* but equally recalled the fetal movements in their womb.

The women who remembered their children's prenatal behavior freely gave me of their time and information. Some started saying that "come to think of it, the babies were pretty much of the same type when I carried them that they were when they ran around on their own."

I only wish I had a larger number of subjects, once the women who did not recall the gestational period were eliminated from the sample. In any case, mine is a replicable experiment and my readers may even enjoy doing so.

Results

A total of seventy-five women, fifty Americans and twenty-five Japanese, confirmed my hypothesis. After they described the behavior of their children in the womb and the behavior of these same children as babies and toddlers, the continuity of the personality traits became clearly established.

There was only one exception: an American mother said that both her girl and her boy were very active in the womb, but now both are shy and quiet and like reading best. Basically, my hypothesis was confirmed, but I have no explanation for the two cases which disproved it unless there was something in these siblings' emotional or educational system that made them become so quiet. Their parents are divorced, but so were others in my sample.

The quiet versus the lively personality

This answer was particularly revealing. As said above, I made sure that my question was not loaded. Three women, when I asked whether their children had different personalities, like some being more active and others more of the quiet type, answered in wording similar to that of a thirty-year-old American mother: "My two children are different and the difference was already apparent in the womb. They showed the same behavior before and after birth."

Another woman said that her son "kicked hard and is the same after birth. He is the outgoing type." A mother of four said, "One of my children used to kick so hard that I thought I would get a broken rib." Later on in the interview, she came back to this child to tell me that: "Of all my six children, this is by far the most rambunctious and energetic."

One mother of three boys said "The first and the third kicked hard and now they are very active and outgoing. The second one was so quiet when I was pregnant that up until the fifth month I did not even know I was pregnant. Now the second one is a complete introvert, very quiet. He likes to do his own thing while my third one is a showman."

The mother of two girls told me that her first one "was more active in the womb and is now the more active type." Her second one "kicked less and is now very reserved."

A young mother of two characterized them in the following manner: "My nine-month-old tries to get my attention by agitating her hands. When she is picked up she will quiet down. When I was carrying her, she would kick until I caressed my abdomen and then she would cease moving." This child's pre- and postnatal behavior will also be reported in the section on music, below.

One mother of four is convinced that there is a behavioral difference between boys and girls. Research has not confirmed this belief which seems widely held. As brought out in the chapter on predicting the sex of an expected child, the majority of cultures attribute more forceful movements to the male fetus while only a minority believe the female is more active. The findings presented here justify no difference between the sexes. This is also asserted by the obstetrician consulted in chapter ten on "What the pregnant woman can do to assure physical and mental health for her child."

This same woman told me that she used to touch her abdomen when she was pregnant and that she was very attentive because, even though she had four live births she also had three miscarriages and remembered her pregnancies quite well. She said that "the three boys were very active before birth and are very active now. The girl was very quiet in the womb and is the quiet type now." The mother was so sure she was expecting a girl that she "did all her knitting in pink."

A very clear-cut answer came from the mother of five boys. I asked her first whether she recalled the behavior of her children in the womb and she remembered right away that "the first kicked little and was a breach birth, the second kicked a lot, the third was the liveliest of them all, the fourth and fifth were laid-back." Then I asked how they are now and she said immediately that they are exactly like they were in the womb: "The third one has the highest metabolism, is the most active, moves around all the time. He also has the most active mind." I then told her that this confirms my hypothesis and she said: "Of course, how could it be otherwise?"

One mother of two girls and one boy said that the boy was extremely active in the womb and is so now. I know the child and he is a real fireball. One of her girls was so quiet that she started worrying, until her doctor confirmed that there was nothing wrong. Now this girl just likes to read and sit quietly by herself.

The mother of two boys told me that her first one was very quiet in the womb but was hyperactive after birth. He is now cured and doing well. I excluded all similar cases from my survey report because my research is limited to the perfectly normal in order not to introduce any extraneous variables. Her other son was "pretty active" during gestation. He was born two weeks late. "He is always stubborn and just did not want to come out," his mother commented.

Another mother said that her middle child was very active in the womb and "moved like a wave." He is now the most gregarious of her children.

One woman remarked that the child of hers that moved actively in the womb is now the outgoing type while the other one that moved very little has a shy personality.

Another mother, originally from Finland, reported about her two girls that the first one was very quiet in the womb while the second one was quite active. Now the first one likes to listen to stories told in a soft voice while the second one jumps up and down and does not behave unless her mother "scolds her with a loud voice."

One mother's second child moved so much that she "felt pain and had difficulties in getting to sleep." He is now a very outgoing type "who leaves too large a tip when eating out." Her other son was more quiet in the womb and is now a very considerate young man "who plans everything carefully."

Another mother had three boys, all very active during gestation and all three very active children now. The same was reported by a mother of three girls.

A mother of four remembered her second child because he was stronger and was active in her womb. "And now he is a boxer," she added.

One father, who happens to be a child psychiatrist and who was strongly involved in the pregnancies of his wife, told me that "all four children were very active in the womb. Now they are all go-getters."

Sleeping patterns

Several women mentioned the sleeping pattern of their children and brought out that these were established in the womb and continued after birth. This information was fully volunteered as I made no mention of sleeping patterns when I talked to my respondents. This is what one mother said about her five-month-old son: "When I started relaxing to go to sleep, the baby in my womb started moving and then relaxed too. I guess he went to sleep. It was always around 10:00 p.m. Now this is his feeding time and then we go to sleep."

Another mother said of her three children that the boy seemed to sleep less in the womb than her girls. He used to wake her up early in the morning by kicking hard. "He is now an early riser while the girls let me sleep while I was pregnant and don't bother me now."

A mother of two boys told me that her first one slept less and used to kick so hard she "felt the pain in the ribs." Now when nap time comes, she "has to order him to go to rest." The other one who slept more in the womb, "will go for his blanket all by himself and be happy to have a rest."

One mother of two boys and a girl remembered only one thing about her three "miraculous pregnancies." They all were lively and "no good sleepers." Now that her children are adults, they are *all* healthy and energetic professionals.

One boy who was very active in the womb, and according to his mother, never seemed to sleep now has difficulties going to sleep. His brother slept adequately in the womb and "now sleeps regularly and is very easy to care for."

Musical inclination

Mention of a child's liking for music was spontaneous as I made no mention of it during the interviews. The interesting fact about this finding is that the mothers compared it with their children's other likes and desires. This lends itself particularly well to my comparison of the child's prenatal and its postnatal behavior.

A woman recalled that during gestation, her two sons were very different. One preferred for her to "caress her abdomen while the other one favored music. After birth, one child wanted to be picked up and the other one preferred music."

One mother was very specific. She likes to sing when she cooks and works around the house. Her second child used to move around the womb with the musical rhythm of her mother's singing and now she often sings by herself. The other girl is "not much musically inclined and just craves for companionship."

Another mother was equally specific telling me that one of her girls used to "dance in her belly" when mother and father went to a concert. She now plays the piano and listens to music all the time. Her other children were equally exposed to music during gestation, but their reaction was not so intense.

Still another mother remarked that two boys among her children seemed to particularly like it when she played music while she was pregnant and both now play the piano.

One child, still another mother told me, seemed to like music very much during gestation, and now dances and plays the piano.

One mother constantly played music to her three children during pregnancy. Two seemed to like it and they sing now. The third one was very active in the womb but without relation to the music and now does not particularly care for music either.

A mother of four told me that her oldest child was very receptive to music during gestation. As an infant, "she sang before she talked."

Conclusion

If all this has not convinced the reader that our individual personality is formed while we are still in our mother's womb, I would like him/her to contact me with evidence to the contrary.

By the early formation of the basic personality type I do not mean that within each type there are not variations and changes over time. This book, indeed, has shown that beyond the predictable growth of the brain depending on its genes and the nourishment necessary for a healthy, full deployment of its mental capacities, the fetus also profits from active cerebral stimulation. In other words, the fetus is capable of learning.

In chapter two I have presented the medical evidence that the fetal brain has the necessary capabilities for receiving, storing, and reacting to external stimuli. And by external stimuli I mean that the fetus is aware of what goes on outside the womb.

If the fetus becomes familiar with a musical theme that is played consistently, after birth it will recognize this theme as distinct from other musical tones. It is well established that the neonate can distinguish its mother's voice from that of others. Where the father was consistently involved in interacting with the child his wife carried in her womb, I know of cases where the neonate also recognized its father's voice.

Before I end this chapter, I want to assert again that I am not talking in Freudian terms. I see the intra-uterine period of human life as an integral part of the child's overt development, not radically different from later periods of life.

References

Chamberlain, D. (1988). *Babies remember birth*. New York: Ballantine Books.

Liley, W. (1972). The foetus as a personality. *Australian & New Zealand Journal of Psychiatry*, 6, 99–105.

Questionnaire for Our Individual Personality

Name: . . . .
Country of origin and place of birth: . . . .
Date of birth: . . . .   Marital Status: . . . .
Address and telephone number: . . . .
. . . .
(This is only for in case I need further information. No names
will be used in the tabulation of the results.)
Place and date of interview: . . . .
Age and sex of children, listed in order of birth. . . . .
. . . .

1. Describe in some detail the diverse personalities of each of your children.
2. Is he/she quiet or loud?
3. Is he/she rambunctious or sedentary?
4. Does he/she like music?
5. How did you interact with each child when he/she was in your womb?
6. Were your children exposed to music before or after birth?
7. Did each of your children behave differently when he/she was in your womb?
8. Were some more quiet while others kicked more forcefully? Did some kick more frequently?

Enculturation Begins Before Birth

Introduction

The question I have presented throughout this book is one that has not yet been broadly raised even though it is a vital issue I have tried to tackle for many years since starting to do research in prenatal behavior thirty years ago (von Raffler-Engel 1964). The salient point of prenatal research for the linguist, the psychologist and the anthropologist is the interaction between the fetus and its mother (von Raffler-Engel 1964, p. 75). The necessary underpinning of such research is the bio-medical evidence which documents the neural development of the fetus (see Chapter 2).

Medical research shows ever more convincingly how active a fetus is even during the first trimester of gestation. Brain waves can be registered at twelve weeks after conception. A miscarriage of less than six months can be viable and a one-pound newborn can be helped to survive. Surgery is possible in utero.

From the social science perspective, the theoretical underpinning of the data I will present is the assumption that communication is verbal and nonverbal from its inception phylogenetically, as well as ontogenetically during the prenatal stage of human development (von Raffler-Engel 1983, pp. 296–308).

The assertion that enculturation begins in the womb is sustained by the documented capability of the fetus to perceive the external environment that surrounds its mother wherever she goes. The child thus lives within its culture before it is born (von Raffler-Engel 1988a, p. 101). After centuries of neglect, we are coming back to recognize the active life of the child in the period before its birth. In olden times this was an accepted fact, as legends and folktales amply attest (von Raffler-Engel 1989).

Culture

Before dealing with the acquisition of culture by the child during its earliest development, I may be permitted to define culture as I see it. I started to say that I would look at culture in its relation to communication when I realized that such a statement is largely redundant. Except when we are totally alone, sleeping on a futon or high up on a mattress, culture is communication. Our behavior communicates to the in-group that we are part of it and to the out-group that we do not share identical presuppositions.

Dictionaries of the social sciences abound in definitions of "culture." The subject is complex because the many sub-cultures of each culture share sets of common features on their own. The classic example is the corporate culture which varies greatly among the capitalist countries but within the uniform purpose of producing money for the firm.

With regard to my thesis that the enculturation of the child begins during its intra-uterine stage, the relevant sub-culture is the family. But this by no means excludes the culture-at-large of the environment where the mother is living. Except when she lives in a harem, a pregnant woman goes about her daily routines of shopping, visiting friends, etc. Her fetus is thus exposed to the community-at-large beyond its immediate family.

The auditory faculty

As pointed out earlier in this book, it is well established in physics that sound travels through water and thus outside noises can reach the fetus through the amniotic fluid. Bio-medical research has documented that "the auditory system is functional by the start of the third trimester" of pregnancy (Birnholz & Benaceraff 1983, note 5). These authors have observed a startle effect to noise in a fetus at 25 weeks of gestation. Indeed, between 26 and 40 weeks of gestational age, the fetal reaction to acoustic stimuli demonstrates "a functional maturation of the central nervous system" (Gagnon et al. 1987 p. 1375). The cochlear function is "present at the fifth month of gestation" (Sadovsky et al. 1986). Other researchers date the fetal response to auditory stimuli even one week earlier (Westgren et al. 1987).

Maternal responses were tested at the Karolinska Institute at Danderyd Hospital in Sweden where the mothers of healthy fetuses felt a kick immediately after the auditory stimulation (Westgren et al. 1987). I tested this myself in 1960 to be certain that the fetal reaction to outside noise is not induced through the hormonal reaction to the mother's shock or feeling of apprehension caused by a loud noise. Looking out of a window and seeing a big truck and hearing the noise such a vehicle makes does not cause a fearful reaction in a woman but will cause a startling movement in her fetus.

A young American woman who talked to her fetus remarked to me that after birth, her baby was more attuned to her voice than any other. It is indeed known that when a newborn is placed between two women who will speak at the same time and the baby can hear them but cannot see them, it will turn toward its mother (Brazelton and Tronik 1980). The newborn is familiar with its mother's voice from the time it lived in her womb and, therefore, "newborns prefer their mothers voices" (De Casper & Fifer 1980). Bonding does not come about in a few tender moments after birth but is formed in the months-long contact between the mother and the child in her womb.

It is well-known that a fetus will kick nervously when it senses an altercation in the environment. Folk wisdom has known this forever and all cultures advise fathers to keep their pregnant wife "happy," in quiet surroundings. That children exposed to certain musical themes during the gestational period will recognize these themes after birth is by now a well-documented fact.

When I first mentioned this over thirty years ago, only old country women would believe me. Now it is considered sophisticated to expose the unborn to classical music. Women used to sing to their child in the womb. In these modern times, pregnant women attach devices to their body that produce soothing noises for the fetus. We have come full circle, except that, like most of communication among adults which is now by voice mail or other mechanical devices, mothers use electronics to provide "quality" time. This is one more way the child is enculturated into the modern world.

There are great cultural differences in the way mothers interact with the child they are carrying. At the present time, many Oriental mothers will talk to the child in their womb, read aloud and play music for it. Western mothers do some of this, but most do it in a perfunctory manner. While Japanese women do so with dedication and take pleasure in it, most Western women I interviewed expose their child to music or talk to it "because the doctor said to do so." Most do not stop to think whether it is actually purposeful or not and some do not even believe that "it makes any difference at all." A couple of women said they "felt like talking to plants."

Instinctively, albeit unconsciously, women may be aware of the capability of the child in their womb to hear outside noises because they try to avoid places where altercations are taking place. They likely feel the nervous movements of their fetus even though many may not acknowledge them. Most women calm the fetus with their caressing hands although few women mention this. Some Western women, however, are conscious of the fetal auditory powers. A thirty-year-old mother of one child born in 1988 told Diane Allen, one of my researchers, that she did not talk to the child she was carrying even though the doctor had told her to do so, "because it would hear her voice when she talked to everybody else and wouldn't know the difference" between speech directed to the child or to others.

The capacity of the fetus to hear has important implications for the prenatal enculturation of the child. Of course, the fetus does not understand the propositional or illocutionary meaning of what is said. But it gets accustomed to the sounds and the sound patterns of a specific language. Later on, it is likely to feel more comfortable when surrounded by speakers of the familiar language than by foreigners. Bilingual ambiences probably accustom the child to two sound patterns. Being raised bilingual after birth certainly does not present a problem.

Most obvious is the impact of intonation because the intonational rhythm is reinforced by the rhythm of the bodily movements of the mother. This is probably the reason why the mastery of intonation is the hardest aspect of foreign language learning and why incorrect intonation causes more misunderstandings than any other feature of discourse.

Body rhythm

Intonation is also tied to body rhythm which is among the crucial facets of the cross-cultural encounter, if not the most crucial one. This is an area which still needs considerable research. I broached it in a fairly extensive article and thus will mention it here only briefly. Each culture has it own characteristic body rhythm while "rhythmic interactional synchrony is a precondition for successful communication" (von Raffler-Engel 1988 a, pp. 88–90). The problem is compounded by the fact that differences in body rhythm tend to be felt as an irritant the cause of which is hard to identify.

The fetus is enculturated into its mother's body rhythm when she walks or bends or sits down. After birth, the baby will be carried around in its mother's arms. It is known that babies keep the same sleeping rhythm as their mothers. The children of waitresses wake up late and the children of bakers wake up in the early morning hours (von Raffler-Engel 1988 b, p. 302). It is plausible that the same applies before birth.

Body rhythm also influences behavioral forms in which people vary greatly. Chinese men walk with small strides while Americans walk with large strides. An Oriental and a Westerner will cover the same distance in the same amount of time but with a different number of strides. This has nothing to do with the height of the person or the size of the feet. I have compared very tall Chinese with small size Americans and the manner of walking proved strictly cultural.

Discourse rules

Coming back to communicative interaction, what the child learns about discourse rules before it is born is the ratio of silence to speaking during conversation. Mothers that read aloud to stimulate the child in their womb also give it an idea of the ratio of silence and speaking in a lecture. Cultures vary greatly. The Japanese intersperse what they say with frequent short pauses to give the listeners time to fully absorb what they have heard.

Americans do not understand the purpose of these moments of silence. When they want to give their listener a reprieve, they stray from the argument introducing a little joke or some remarks about the pleasantness of the meeting. Such extraneous disruptions leave the Japanese listener at a loss.

The child in the womb also familiarizes itself with the level of loudness of its native tongue. Southern Italians enunciate more forcefully what they have to say than do Britishers. Being familiar with all these linguistic features undoubtedly facilitates the child's language acquisition after birth. While in the womb, it already has been exposed to the supra-segmentals.

Except for the teeth and the descent of the larynx, the vocal tract is formed in the fetus. The mobility of the tongue is operant at an early fetal age. Among the folktales reported in chapter three there are numerous legends of "babies crying from the womb." In those legends, fetuses actually speak in clearly understandable sentences. This is, of course, impossible, but audible cries are attested by physicians during delivery when an adequate amount of air can enter the birth canal. During twin births, the second twin may be heard before it emerges after the first twin has been born (Parvianen 1949). Whether one can distinguish the nationality of a baby from hearing its cry is still debated. The experiments are inconclusive.

Nonverbal behavior, paralanguage, and music

Communication is bi-modal, but the nonverbal mode is more easily apparent in the fetus than the verbal mode. Communication is propositional and illocutionary but mostly the later. The illocutionary act is also the one developed earliest in child language (von Raffler-Engel 1964, p. 37). In the prenatal stage it can be ascertained by the end of the first trimester.

Over the years, I have collected innumerable testimonials from mothers who caressed their abdomen when they felt their child's quickening. This caused the child to quiet down, but when they ceased caressing, the quickening resumed. It is apparent that the child realized that it can obtain what it wants through its kicking movements. The fetus seems aware of the stimulus/response reaction.

Nonverbal communication is the only active means at the disposal of the unborn child. But movement is not all the fetus reacts to and not all the fetus elicits. As said above, the child in the womb has the capacity to hear outside noises.

Several of the women I interviewed reported that their unborn child apparently enjoyed their singing. It would kick and then when the mother started singing, it would become quiet. When she stopped singing, the child would elicit resumption of the singing by returning to kick. The same behavior was observed for music.

What all this implies is that while still in the womb, the child is enculturated to the spoken language and the type of musical rhythm common in its culture. In the nonverbal field, the impact of maternal behavior is clear. It is not known what the differences — if any — are in regard to the manner in which mothers from diverse backgrounds caress their abdomen.

Personality differences in the prenatal stage

There is no doubt in my mind that the fetus manifests a personality of its own as "each fetus develops its own pattern of activity" (Rayborn 1987, p. 899). The next chapter will demonstrate that the child's individual personality as formed in the womb continues stable after birth. Here I will report briefly only on what proves relevant to my thesis that enculturation begins before birth.

Two women, one American and one Japanese, that used to sing when they were pregnant observed that one unborn child would kick when they ceased singing and would calm again when they resumed. Their other child seemed to insist on their caressing the abdomen. As infants and toddlers these children would enjoy music and sing on their own. Their other children were neither as interested in music nor as sensitive to it. The children that loved music were able to sing in tune, the others were not.

It is known that musical ability is hereditary and thus per se has nothing to do with enculturation. What is related to culture is the type of music and, even more so, the rhythmic patterning of the language to which the child is exposed before it is born. Of course, enculturation continues after birth, but this has hardly been challenged. What I want to establish is the continuum of enculturation throughout life, beginning in the womb.

This book adopts my previous theory about early learning which proposes two periods of learning, the prenatal and the post-natal period, one following the other in a continuum. Learning in utero is distinct from inheritance (von Raffler-Engel 1988, p. 101) and should not be confused with the psychological concept of pseudo-inheritance. Culture is not transmitted by genes but learned. Much of it is learned through osmosis. During the pre-natal period all learning comes about in this manner. But not all that is learned is offered without purpose. Reading and playing music for an unborn child is a form of teaching.

Language change after birth

Children inherit the physical features of their natural parents, but if they are raised where another language from that of their parents is spoken, they will acquire the language of their environment. They will also acquire the nonverbal manners of the culture in which they grow up.

There is no data on how an adopted baby feels when it is in the arms of a loving adoptive mother but one that walks and moves and talks in a manner totally different from what the baby was accustomed to before birth. Even the children of immigrants do not show any special aptitude in learning the language of their grandparents. So far, there is no contradiction with what I said before. An unborn child, or a baby for that matter, does not understand the words that are spoken around it and has not yet acquired any rules of grammar.

It is extremely difficult for Americans to master the tones of the Chinese language. Children of American missionaries that have grown up in China can speak like natives. The problem raised by my studies that needs to be researched in this connection is whether children of parents who speak a tone language and are raised by parents who speak a stress language may have less difficulties than others when learning a tone language later in life.

It is also not known whether children whose natural parents practice an expansive gestural system and who are raised in a culture where gestures are close to the body will find it easier to acquire the gestural system of Southern Italy than children of British descent. I am not talking of heredity but of the habituation during the prenatal stage.

What would research in these areas accomplish? Will it be possible to find out how long the prenatal habituation will last when it is superseded by other forms of behavior after birth? Should American women planning to adopt Vietnamese or Brazilian babies study the movements of women in the child's country of origin? And if they so did, what purpose would their study fulfill? I hope my studies do not lend support to those in the United States who oppose adoption across the color line.

For the time being, what I would like to stimulate is pure research. Why is it harder to gain proficiency in certain aspects of communicative behavior than in others when studying a foreign language? It seems that intonation is not only difficult to master when studying a foreign language, it also is the most frequent cause of misinterpretations. This is usually accounted for because linguistic intonation is intertwined with emotional intonation. I would venture to say that the rhythm of language is more profoundly radicated in one's first language than other features because it was acquired before birth.

A foreign speaker can gain perfect mastery over vocabulary and syntax and write with a native proficiency. It is well-known that after puberty, it is rare for an individual to gain native-like pronunciation. This, I believe, is due to the consolidation of the habits of the vocal tract which at puberty reaches its full development. Like vocabulary and syntax, phonation is not acquired before birth. In this connection, it is interesting to notice that having a foreign accent does not generally create severe misunderstandings.

Body odor

That which is acquired before birth might constitute the most integral part of our sense of self, and eventually of our sense of belonging to an in-group. In my research on involuntary clashes in cross-cultural encounters I found that odor plays an important role. Somehow we know this, but the subject seems taboo and has not been adequately researched.

In the fetus the sense of smell develops during the seventh month of conceptual age (Monie 1983, p. 25). Neonates were believed to have a poor sense of smell until recent research proved the contrary. Babies are accustomed to their mother's balm.

As body odor varies greatly among cultures, due in part to their diverse diets, familiarity with the olfaction of the in-group is one more aspect of cultural identity and one more subtle means for the exclusion of the out-group. Tribal allegiance and prejudice are formed in the womb and are thus deeply ingrained and hard to overcome.

The question is: Should they be overcome? Can it be done? If so, how is it possible to go beyond the surface? The answer, as I see it, is that if it does not lead to vicious prejudice (and most prejudice is quite vicious), tribal allegiance is not wrong by definition.

As I pointed out in earlier articles on cross-cultural communication, we cannot — and we may not want to — change ourselves. The key to harmonious communication across cultural barriers is the consciousness of our differences and a positive attitude toward the worth of that which is different. What we need to do is gain ever more knowledge of where we differ. As the old saying goes, the truth will make us free. Understanding that some of our cultural differences start in the womb might make us more tolerant of them.

Prenatal learning as self-defense

As the child matures inside the womb to get ready to function in the outside world after birth, it learns not only how to satisfy its needs by eliciting singing or a caressing response through kicking.

The child also gets ready to interact not only with its mother, but also with the other people that will surround it.

It's a hostile world for a helpless little human being. In the so-called advanced societies, a child is lucky if it does not get killed by abortion. In the so-called underdeveloped countries, during periods of famine, newborn babies may be killed for food. In India, it may get killed before or after birth if it is of the wrong sex. All this is done to the child by its own significant others.

The precarious situation of this tiny, defenseless creature could be even more perilous if it did not bond with its mother through the prenatal recognition of her touch and her voice. As the child grows up, it will be inconspicuous because it easily fits into its culture. This is accomplished by its adjustment to the body motions and the intonation contour of its in-group.

All this is learned before birth as enculturation begins in the womb. Thus, at birth, the child is already a member of its community. Its precocious enculturation is part of the child's defense mechanism after birth. Before birth, the child's defense mechanism works on two planes. Physically, against neglect and exposure to harsh noises or being hit, the fetus is somewhat protected by being surrounded by the water of the amniotic fluid.

The psychological defense against the danger of death by abortion is the child's ability to interact with its mother through quickening. Many women I have interviewed feel that kicking is the child's way to tell them "I am here, I am alive and well." Bonding often dates from that moment. Women are more reluctant to undergo abortion after they have actually felt the movements of their child and its reaction to stroking and singing. The end of the third trimester is also the time when the brain waves of the fetus are developed to the point it is most likely that the fetus can feel pain.

In summary, the child is exposed to the culture of its community while it is still in the womb. There it already starts assimilating the culture-specific movements and intonation contours of its culture. Thus, when it is born and starts growing up, it behaves like a member of the group, minimizing any potential hostility toward the little newcomer.

Last, but not least, let me also say that the early enculturation of the human offspring helps to assure the survival of the race. If children were not accepted and cared for, the human species could not continue.

References

Birnholz, J.C. & Benaceraff, B.R. (1983). The development of human fetal hearing. *Science*, 222 (4623), 516–518.

Brazelton, T.T. & Tronik, E. (1980). Preverbal communication between mothers and infants. In D.R. Olsen (Ed.), *The social foundation of language and thought. Essays in honor of Jerome S. Bruner* (pp. 299–315). New York: Norton.

De Casper, A.J. & Fifer, W.P. (1980). Of human bonding: Newborns prefer their mothers' voices. *Science*, 208, 1174–1176.

De Vries, J.I.P., Visser, G.H.A. & Prechtl, H.F.R. (1988). The emergence of fetal behavior III. Individual differences and consistencies. *Early Human Development*, 16, 85–103.

Gagnon, R., Hunse, C., Carmichael, L., Fellows, F. & Patrick, J. (1987). Human fetal responses to vibratory acoustic stimulation from twenty-six weeks to term. *American Journal of Obstetrics and Gynecology*, 157, 1375–1381.

Monie, I.W. (1983). Development and physiology of the fetus. In A.B. Garbie & J.G. Sciarra (Eds.), *Gynecology and obstetrics* (Vol. 2, rev ed., chapter 5). Philadelphia, PA: Harper & Row.

Parvianen, S. (1949). Vagitus uterinus. *Annales Chirurgiae et Gynecologiae Fenniae*, 38, 330–336.

Rayburn, W.E. (1987). Monitoring fetal body movement. *Clinical Obstetric Investigation*, 21, 177–181.

Sadovsky, E., Samueloff, A., Sadovsky, Y. & Ohel, G. (1986). Incidence of spontaneous and evoked fetal movement. *Gynecologic and Obstetric Investigation*, 21, 177–181.

von Raffler-Engel, W. (1964). *Il prelinguaggio infantile* Brescia: Paideia (Studi grammaticali e linguistici 7).

von Raffler-Engel, W. (1983). On the synchronous development of gesticulation and vocalization in man's early communicative behavior. In E. de Grolier (Ed.), *Glossogenetics: The origin and evolution of language* (pp. 295–312) (Proceedings of the Transdiciplinary Symposium on Glossogenetics sponsored by the International Social Science Council, UNESCO, Paris, 1980). Paris: Harwood Academic Press

von Raffler-Engel, W. (1988a). The impact of covert factors in cross-cultural communication. In F. Poyatos (Ed.), *Cross cultural perspectives in nonverbal communication* (pp. 71–104). Toronto: Hogrefe.

von Raffler-Engel, W. (1988b). The synchronous development of language and kinesics: Further evidence. In M.E. Landsberg (Ed.), *Genesis of language: A different judgment of evidence* (pp. 227–246) (Selected papers from the Symposium on Language Origins, XIth International Congress of Anthropological and Ethnological Sciences, University of British

Columbia, 1983). Berlin: Mouton de Gruyter (Studies in Anthropological Linguistics 3).

von Raffler-Engel, W. (1989). *Further evidence of verbal and non-verbal communication between the mother and her unborn child in the womb — in support of the author's theory of the bi-model origin of language.* Vth Annual Meeting of the Language Origins Society, University of Texas at Austin. To be published by John Benjamins.

Wedenberg, E. (1965). Prenatal tests of hearing. *Acta Otolarynogologica*, Supplement 207, 27.

Westgren, M., Alstron, H., Nyman, M. & Ulmsten, U. (1987). Maternal perception of sound-provoked fetal movements as a measure of fetal well-being. *British Journal of Obstetrics and Gynecology, 94,* 523–527.

From Prenatal Communication to Adult Language: The Prelinguistic Stage

Language develops before birth

Up to now, this book has been concerned with the communicative abilities of the child before its birth. It has attempted to show that there is communication between the unborn child and its mother and that the unborn child is responsive to stimuli, like light and noise, that come from the surroundings beyond the maternal womb. The fetal response to outside stimuli is direct and not merely transmitted through the emotion experienced by its mother.

As the fetus matures, his powers of perception and reaction increase. His capacity for learning during the prenatal stage is proven by the recognition a baby demonstrates during delivery and after birth for a musical theme that was consistently played in the presence of its mother during gestation.

People tend to look at me in amazement when I talk about the distinction I make between a prenatal and a postnatal period of learning. They question my terminology and assume that prenatal learning is nothing else than the maturational development of instinctual behavior. I hope this book will clarify my concept of an active learning involvement in the fetus. I have also attempted to show the stimulating function of the mother and of the broader external environment on the evolving intelligence of the unborn child.

In this book communication is viewed as a continuum from its inception during the prenatal period to its final stage before the death of the communicator. Like all other vital functions and activities, the power to communicate follows a normal growth curve and has peaks and valleys. Eventually, there may be a decline before death due to diseases such as Alzheimer's. Within its biological framework shared by all humans, the style in which the fetus, the baby, the infant, and finally the adult communicate is culture-specific. It involves learning.

Within the broad context of communication, language seems to be the most highly developed form. It allows for the greatest specificity and can span over time, from the remote past to the distant future. Language has fixed, albeit not immutable, rules on the level of sound as well as form. It takes no less than ten years of life to master the complexities of grammar.

As I said in the first chapter, linguists disagree on when to date the onset of language. Many linguists do not study language as part of a total system of communication and opt for treating it as an entity all its own. Some even believe that communication is a late adjunct to the function of language (Swiggers 1988). They do not study babies and certainly do not take into consideration the period before the baby's birth. My own perspective views language as part of communication. I consider language a refinement of more rudimentary forms of communication rather than their replacement. As I see it, language does not supersede some primitive forms of expression, but enriches communication through additional forms that allow for more detail as the human being matures and can cope with greater specificity and go beyond the here and now.

Scientific tests for prenatal language awareness

Recent brain research lends credence to my earlier assertion that the learning of language initiates in the womb. Thirty years ago, I tested the reaction of babies to the sound of regular language as opposed to the sound of nonsense syllables by observing the behavior of babies lying in their crib. When friendly adults approached them and talked to them in the customary high pitched "baby talk" which involves simple, repetitive sentences but normal words, the babies looked at the adult and made responsive noises. Often they cried when the visitor left them. On the contrary, babies approached by equally friendly adults who would talk to them in arbitrary sound sequences elicited much less interest and the babies seldom, if ever, complained when left alone (von Raffler-Engel 1964, pp. 23–24).

How did these babies distinguish between a linguistically correct sound sequence and one that did not adhere to the rules of their mother tongue? My answer is that they were familiar with the regular language and felt comfortable with it. When did they learn to recognize the difference? At this time, scientific research is not yet completely equipped to fully support my belief that the difference is learned during the intra-uterine stage. I cannot incontrovertibly prove my assertion, but I can adduce a biological argument that strongly supports it.

The adult brain reacts differently when presented with words that follow the acceptable sound sequence of the subject's mother tongue than it does when presented with words formed with linguistically unacceptable sound combinations. When a word contains the correct sound combination, the brain will search for its meaning, regardless of whether this word actually has meaning in the language. The presentation of a word with an unacceptable sound sequence does not elicit any semantic search (Begley et al. 1992, p. 68). PET scans show that certain clusters of neurons on the left side of the brain light up only when the words presented follow the correct sound combination.

The reporters of this research conclude that "since babies aren't born knowing the acceptable sound sequences, the brain must have learned these rules." The report does not mention the possibility of prenatal learning. I venture to say that when a baby is born, it is already familiar with the language spoken around it. Like its recognition of musical themes as opposed to less familiar tunes, a baby recognizes the verbal sound sequences to which it was exposed before its birth and it can distinguish these sequences from novel combinations.

For me, as the basic structure of the brain is formed before birth, there is no reason to doubt that mother tongue recognition predates birth. My hypothesis could be tested on individuals that through adoption were raised in a language different from that of their biological parents. It would also be interesting to observe the reaction of individuals whose mother lived in a completely bilingual environment.

My conclusion is that the acquisition of language begins before birth. This is a very different position from the innateness theory. I mean that language is learned and that learning starts in the womb. Obviously, the fetus' capacity for learning is commensurate with the primitive stage of its development and its limited experience. The newborn child does not understand the word for any object in the outside world. Its grasp for grammatical rules develops much later. What it brings to the world is the knowledge previously acquired about the emotive component of intonation and touch and its habituation to the sounds of the language that was spoken around its mother during gestation. Its habituation may also include musical themes or the cadence of poetry readings if it was exposed to them during the prenatal period. If sensations were not stored in memory, it would be unlikely that a six-month-old fetus could have the rapid eye movements that people display when they are dreaming (National Geographic Society 1992).

The carrier sound

As described in the earlier chapters of this book, during its intrauterine stage the child communicates its emotive needs. At birth, the child is capable of emitting cries. Soon mothers can distinguish intonational variations in the cry for hunger, pain, or desire for companionship. As early as three months of age, in addition to the cry which will persist for more than a year, a baby may already have developed the second means of expression. Cognitively, this is a far more advanced stage of development but still based on melodic variation. He will consistently vary a tonal pattern depending on whether he wants to draw his mother's attention to some object, or actually induce her to get that object for him.

This denotative expression is the earliest form of real language because here the melodic variation is not only musical but accompanies a specific sequence of verbal sounds. When I first documented this pattern, I called this consistent verbal sound the "carrier sound" because its function is to carry the melodic pattern in which the meaning resides (von Raffler-Engel 1964). Many infants I observed had sounds like a prolonged vocalic *m*, or a repetitive *u*, or *bu* and *bu-bu*, and *da* (Ibid., pp. 92–93). The carrier sound is simply a sound that is easy for the infant to pronounce at will. The sound being consistent, it requires conscious articulation. This is why it is the earliest form of language, pre-language.

Language is verbal and nonverbal

The carrier sound, more often than not, is accompanied by the pointing gesture. Although the pointing gesture has been recognized by some modern linguists, theories of language acquisition mostly ignore the fact that language is not only vocal, but also gestural. The sign language of the deaf, as symbolically complex as it may be, is not the normal form in which the healthy human expresses himself. A written text is only verbal, but it incorporates the nonverbal component descriptively, like saying "he smiled with both eyes." In the natural context there is no purely verbal communication. If we point in a certain direction, we need not indicate this direction in verbal terms. Even people as kinesically quiet as Englishmen shrug their shoulders and use facial expression. The Japanese are keen observers of nonverbal communication. As they say, "Hear one and understand ten."

If we focus exclusively on the verbal mode, we construct linguistic theories that are not based on reality. In the womb and after birth, communication is bi-modal and when we study the language development of the child we must take this into account. The visual and the auditory mode are more closely related than is commonly supposed. Ten years ago, I had a student of mine video-tape conversation between a series of blind men. We were amazed to see each time that they coordinated their gestural behavior and body posturing just like seeing people do. The explanation I gave at the time was that they sensed the displacement of air caused by the movements of their conversation partner and reacted in syn-chrony just as seeing people do. The latter also do not really look at the movements of their partner and the mutual adjustment is virtually synchronous. Recent computer research has shown that a computer can reconstruct the contours of undersea obstacles from the "subtle fluctuations in the natural sound that permeates the ocean" (Browne 1992).

Expressive and receptive language

In the verbal as well as in the nonverbal mode, communication entails the expressive component of speaking/gesturing as well as the receptive component of understanding orally and visually. In observing children it is clear that they understand before they speak the regular words of adult language. In the pre-language pe-riod, the relationship between the receptive and the expressive form is not so clearly apparent. All babies cry when they are hun-gry. This is instinctual and not by imitation.

Crying is a form of communication, but it is not language and as language develops, crying will gradually recede. There is never-theless an element of learning in crying behavior. Babies like to be picked up and when they find out that crying gets the desired result, they will cry whenever they wish to be picked up. If they are not regularly picked up when they cry, they will discontinue crying for that purpose. The baby's crying behavior resembles his kicking behavior during the fetal stage when he wanted to elicit caressing movements.

It is when the child reaches the stage of the carrier sound that we can speak of the onset of regular language. Although melodic variation is still the carrier of meaning, the consistency of the phonological component, as in a word, can be considered the beginning of regular language. We can say that in the ontogeny of language, tonal language is the earliest form of language in the developing child. Phylogenetically, it may very well be that this replicates the remote origin of human language. There are still many tonal languages, like Chinese, and it is likely that Indo-European was a tonal language before it became a stress language.

The carrier sound is like a word as it has the basic features of adult language in as much as it is willfully articulated with a consistent phonological pattern. It may have one or two syllables, like *da* or *da-da*. The phonological pattern is still devoid of meaning and only a carrier for the tonal variation. The pointing gesture that often accompanies the carrier sound still does not have the culture-specific forms of pointing. Like the carrier sound, it is not the result of imitation. In adult tone languages, like Chinese, the baby will learn to master the tones as well as the phonology. In non-tonal languages, like English and Japanese, he will only have to learn the phonological patterning of the words. In all languages, he will have to learn the correct intonational pattern of the sentence.

In the stage of the carrier sound, production seems to precede comprehension. As I said above, I prefer to consider the carrier sound a rudimentary form of discourse rather than a word or a one-word sentence. A three-month-old infant appears to understand simple discourse, but this cannot yet be scientifically proven. Soon thereafter imitation begins; and comprehension precedes production from then on. As the infant gains teeth he can produce a variety of sounds and gradually imitate adult words. His gestural behavior will also become culture-specific as he copies adult gestures, such as waving good-bye with the palm of the hand or the back of the hand showing, depending on whether his environment is German or Italian.

The stage when the infant starts imitating adult language is called the holophrastic or one-word sentence stage, a term I do not share. What this term implies is that the infant may say one word but with the intention of a whole sentence. I prefer to think that these first imitative utterances are not really one-word sentences. What the child does is pick up the word or word combination that seems to accomplish the communicative purpose in a manner he can master, like saying an approximation for the word for food in order to get fed.

A classic example for the so-called one-word sentence among American children is *all gone*, which means there is nothing left. In the English language these are two words, *all* meaning everything and *gone* meaning left, finished, or disappeared. Italian children have the equivalent to *all gone*. One of their earliest expressions is *non c' è più*, sometimes reduced to *pu*. In Italian dictionary terms *non c' è più* consists of four words. The child certainly does not have the concept of word and does not seem to distinguish between one word and two words when he combines them in a unit. At that age, he also does not have the concept of sentence. As I see it, the child communicates a message. Discourse precedes the word and the sentence.

What this implies is that the child acquires language going from the broad context to the narrow units. Language acquisition does not begin with the phoneme (that is a single sound characteristic of his native language) nor does it begin with an innate sentence structure from which he derives shorter sentences. For me, he first understands and expresses a communicative message. Only gradually does he master the correct pronunciation and recognize the boundaries of words. The same probably also applies to the acquisition of a foreign tongue when learned spontaneously rather than in the formal teaching context.

While it was in the womb, the child saw only contours when the light was favorable. It could not see its mother. It did hear the noises in its mother's surroundings, including conversations which evidently it did not understand. The recent brain research quoted earlier in this chapter shows that it is possible that the unborn child has become familiar with the sound pattern of the language in which these conversations were conducted. It supports my assertion that language acquisition begins in the intra-uterine period of life.

This puts a great responsibility on the pregnant woman and on the people who talk with her. All folk advice insists that an expecting mother should be addressed in a considerate, calm manner and that no violent, loud altercations should take place in her presence. She should also not go to sad events, like funerals. The reason given is that neither the mother nor her child should be emotionally disturbed.

This is certainly good advice, but it becomes even more important when we consider that the fetus is learning his native language
and that he should not learn speech as a loud, ill-tempered form
of expression. From the recent research reported in this book we
now know that more is involved than emotional calm to benefit
the child in the womb.

Japanese women are advised to read to their unborn child.
Whatever is read to him will not be understood for the content,
but the child will hear a pleasant, well-uttered sequence of sentences. Isn't this the way all parents want their children to talk
eventually? We want to raise them to be calm and well-mannered.
Taikyò will help to accomplish this task.

References

Begley, Sharon; Weight, Linda; Church, Vernon; and Hager, Mary, 1992.
    "Mapping the brain" *Newsweek* vol. CXIX, Nr. 16 (April 20), pp. 66–
    70.
Browne, Malcolm W., 1992. "Using natural sounds, system tries to 'see'
    objects deep in ocean" *The New York Times*, (April 21) pp. C8.
National Geographic Society 1986. *The incredible machine*
Swiggers, P., 1988. Review of Hagege, C., 1985 "L'homme de paroles: Con-
    tribution linguistique aux sciences humaines" (Paris: Fayard). *Language*
    vol. 64, Nr. 1, pp. 188–189.
von Raffler-Engel, Walburga, 1964. *Il prelinguaggio infantile* Brescia:
    Paideia (Studi grammaticali e linguistici 7).

What the Pregnant Woman Can Do to Assure Physical and Mental Health for Her Child

10

Introduction

This book begins with an introduction to acquaint the reader with the perspective in which it presents the needs of the child growing inside its mother's womb. Through medical research and tradition of old, I have attempted to show that the fetus is actively involved in its environment. Like a little child, the unborn demands love and attention. Even when they do not have a word like *taikyó*, mothers all over the world watch out for the needs of their fetus.

The concept of *taikyó* in its ancient meaning was the focus at the beginning of this book and it is again the focus of its final chapter. The beginning was theoretical and anthropological. In this concluding chapter, I may be permitted to offer a little practical advice on how best to follow the precepts of *taikyó*. What good is the purpose of knowing theory and history if not to use this knowledge for the benefits it can bring?

I was trained in linguistics and in anthropology and specialize in cross-cultural communication. Thus, I do not have the authority to offer professional advice to a pregnant woman. To provide valid information to my readers, I consulted with an experienced obstetrician/gynecologist who is sympathetic to my perception of the fetus as a little human being endowed with rudimentary intelligence. The English language does not have the equivalent of the word *taikyó* and Dr. Sarratt was happy to learn about such "a useful word," as he put it.

The Japanese dictionary definition of *taikyó* (Daikawa Jiten, Showa 61, vol. 13, p. 9628) begins with the advice that the woman "should sit straight." Indeed, the mother's good posture allows for the child to move freely in as much room as possible. A crouched position compresses the abdomen reducing the room for the child. This raises the question of whether wearing a pregnancy corset, as is still customary in Japan, is beneficial, harmful, or of no impact.

Posture support

Dr. Sarratt is against wearing such a support because he does not consider it of use to the child and often of discomfort for the mother. In my own pregnancies, I tried several girdles and finally decided not to wear any as they all made me feel uncomfortable. According to Dr. Sarratt there is no need for any corset in a normal pregnancy because the mother can fully support the weight of the child. An American woman told me that wearing a "maternity girdle" made her feel less heavy. That a corset may prevent the woman from slouching has not occurred to be of consideration to any American person I interviewed. I have no statistics to consider the pros and cons of wearing a corset for that purpose. I also cannot judge whether the traditional Japanese ceremony when a woman starts wearing the pregnancy corset is psychologically more beneficial to the mother-to-be or to her mother-in-law.

Diet

The Japanese dictionary definition proceeds mentioning that the woman should "have a correct diet." What is a correct diet? Over time, opinions have differed greatly concerning the quality as well as the quantity of the food. When I was pregnant in the nineteen-fifties and living in New York City, my gynecologist constantly warned me not to gain weight. He advised me to eat as little as possible. But at that time — and fortunately no longer prevalent today — the general concern was less for the welfare of the baby as it was for the elegant looks of the mother. I was earnestly told that "it would be difficult to lose all of the weight gain afterwards and I would look unattractive." I had enough common sense to reject this advice and in good European fashion I ate as much as I felt I needed. I did not, however, force myself to "eat for two," which in earlier times women were supposed to do, forcing themselves to eat more than they really desired. Dr. Sarratt answered my question in this regard, suggesting that a pregnant woman eat as much as she wants, without consideration for weight gain, but certainly not to the point of getting indigestion.

Concerning the quality of the food intake, he suggests that a healthy diet is important at any time, and particularly during gestation. Eating habits differ widely in various countries, but the basics of a healthy diet remain the same, whatever the particulars. Professional dietitians also have different opinions. There is one general agreement which is to avoid much fat. The meat should be lean and the fatty parts of the fish should be cut off.

Everybody needs proteins, carbohydrates, fruits and vegetables. The pregnant woman should make sure she gets the right amount of each of these ingredients in her customary eating habits. It does not matter whether she eats rice or pasta or potatoes as long as her customary habits are integrated into a balanced combination of fresh substance. Needless to say, she should avoid alcohol, but will not be harmed by an occasional glass of wine. The same applies for coffee and black tea. The latest research, as far as I know, attributes benefits to green tea. Of course, nothing is ever good when taken to excess. Everybody knows that drugs are a no-no. Food plays a large part in the folklore of gestation and I have mentioned some of these peculiar practices in the chapter on superstitions.

Smoking

Smoking is definitely harmful and so is the inhalation of smoke from third parties who are smoking. "Passive inhalation" is a complex legal problem. In the United States this problem is being addressed with great earnestness. Women who are addicted to cigarettes should stop before they get pregnant to avoid withdrawal symptoms during their gestation.

Father's diet

More and more research is presently done on the influence of fathers' food intake. In all the cultures I examined it was known that a drunken man may generate a defective baby. Not all cultures consider the fact that even a man who is not drunk at the time of impregnation may have a defective baby if he has a heavy drinking problem. The same applies to drugs.

Emotional state

The next suggestion in the dictionary definition of *taikyó* is "to see no evil." The folk beliefs and many religious injunctions are replete with such advice and I have reported on them in the respective chapters of the book. This is good advice, but, as Dr. Sarratt remarked, how can anybody possibly "see only happy things?" Today's woman works and cannot just stay home throughout her pregnancy. And even if she stays at home, an older child of hers could break an arm and there is not necessarily a mother-in-law to take care of the matter, and maybe not even a neighbor when everybody is out at work. "See no evil" is sound advice but hard to follow in today's world.

But *taikyó* envisions such difficulties when it includes the advice that "during her pregnancy a woman should maintain her mental and emotional calmness and train herself to behave better so that she can provide a favorable influence for her unborn child." (Nihon Kokuga Daijiten, Showa 49, vol. 12, p. 529). Modern psychiatrists might disagree with such Confucian self-control.

Most cultures really advise pregnant women not to have negative thoughts. It seems that all societies are aware that a woman's mood is hormonally transmitted to the child in her womb. This is why they advise family and friends to surround the woman with kindness and, whenever possible, to hide sad events from her. Here, like in everything else, all one can say, is "do the best you can." Life goes on and nothing is perfect. Also, nothing comes without some effort and it may not be unreasonably demanding for a pregnant woman that she concentrate her thoughts on happy things in order to get in a happy mood. Dr. Sarratt suggests she try to do so as much as possible.

He reports that it is known that calmer women have calmer babies. But here the question arises whether this is due to a hereditary factor or to the special circumstances surrounding the pregnancy. Most cultures believe in the latter and this is obviously why they have so many regulations for the behavior of the women themselves and all the people surrounding them. Scientifically, we cannot rule out heredity.

To find an answer to the question we have to compare children by the same woman born after periods of calm and periods of turmoil. Even if we did this research we cannot rule out hereditary factors on the father's side. Like every other aspect of human behavior, a tendency to keep calm is likely to stem from the combination of hereditary and environmental factors. Among the latter are also the societal conventions of self-control versus unhampered free expression. But these may also be among the former because molecular biologists tell me that after hundreds of years, a consistently practiced behavior may become hereditary. From our practical standpoint, all we want to say is that it is in the best interest of the child that the expectant mother be as calm as possible.

Work

Many of today's women work, some by choice and most by necessity. Is work harmful to pregnant women? Virtually all cultures recommend that the expectant mother be helped as much as possible. She is not supposed to lift heavy kitchen pots. She should not get overly tired. There is one exception to this rule: A tribe of American Indians believes that the mother should work harder because this will make her baby strong. This may not sound so strange when compared to modern-day exercise classes where women are urged to work out strenuously so that their muscles will be resilient and flexible during delivery.

Dr. Sarratt recommends that the pregnant woman keep doing what she is accustomed to do but desist if she feels that the work interferes with her increased need for rest and sleep. Of course, all this advice refers to normal pregnancies. If a woman bleeds, she may have to desist from any type of physical activity and lie in bed for several months. Pregnancy complications call for special treatment and have to be dealt with individually.

This book also does not deal with the legal questions of whether women in the age group that might get pregnant should be allowed to work in factories where they are exposed to radiation or chemicals of potential harm to an embryo. I personally find it difficult to understand that the women's movement in the United States of America fought for a women's right to work where she wants to and that the potential hazards to a possible pregnancy are her concern and not that of her employer.

The same women's movement supports maternity leave with pay. What makes this issue even more complex is that a man's exposure to harmful substances in the workplace might equally damage a child he will generate. In my view, the only safe alternative is to clean up our environment. Even if the costs are high, the well-being of the next generation makes it certainly worth our while, and — hopefully — mandatory in the not too distant future.

Marital relations

With regard to sex, cultures vary widely. Some polygamous societies suggest total abstinence during pregnancy. Abstinence is also advised by Orthodox rabbis. Most modern cultures have no regulations at all in this regard. Dr. Sarratt suggests to "do as usual" except for the last month when it could precipitate an early birth. The time of resumption of sex after delivery also varies in different cultures, from almost immediately to a long waiting period. Dr. Sarratt suggests to wait six weeks.

Music

Coming back to the specifics of the dictionary definitions for *taikyó*, the mother-to-be is advised to "listen to good music and suitable counsel in order for her to provide good influence for her unborn child." Listening to good music here seems to refer to the hormonal transmission of a pleasant mood. There is much more to it. It has been documented that after birth, children will recognize a tune played to them during the gestational period and calm down when they hear it.

Many women I interviewed over the years, while preparing this book, told me that their child inside moved rhythmically to the tune of music they were listening to. The child moved even when the mother was calmly seated in a concert hall and did not swing. Many pregnant women sing either for their own pleasure or to entertain the child in their womb.

Medical evidence has shown that the fetus is capable of hearing. Acoustical physics has shown that the sound can be audible through the water. The effect of good music thus is not only on the mood of the mother but also directly on the child she carries. Of course "good music" means quiet rhythm and no excessive loudness. Classical music seems to be the favorite the world over.

Paternal involvement

Many fathers now play music for their expected child. For the fetus who hears the sound, it really makes no difference who plays the music. The question of paternal involvement, however, is an extremely complex one. It is positive for family harmony that the father be part of the process of expecting a child, that he talk about it with the mother and that he help her in whatever she needs. His attitude is psychologically important for the mother. It may also assist the bonding process with the child later on.

There are several cultures like the Kurdish one, where fathers have traditionally touched their wives' abdomens to feel the kicking of their child. Commonly the birthing event is attended by women only, with very few exceptions where the father officially cuts the umbilical cord.

In Western society now there is a new trend and fathers are encouraged to stay in the delivery room and watch the event. Dr. Sarratt tells me that some fathers almost collapse; but some do so even when they are outside, pacing the floor or sitting in the recovery room. Some women want their husbands present and others don't. The decision must be made by the wife, Dr. Sarratt insists.

Speaking of fathers collapsing while their wives give birth, I am reminded of the "courade" practiced by the Black Carib, an American Indian tribe in Belize, Central America. Here the father lies in bed as he is considered to be in need of rest while his wife is up and around (Munroe 1973; Broud 1988, 1989).

From the practical perspective I have taken in this chapter, we are confronted with a vital issue. It remains to be seen whether the father's active involvement in touching his wife's abdomen, playing music and singing for the child, going to prenatal exercise classes with his wife and even participating in those exercises, has a positive effect on the child.

In most societies, the practice is too recent to allow any judgment on its results. Dr. Sarratt remarked that fathers have to be taught to do all these things that come instinctively to mothers. The paternal instinct is one of protection, of providing food and shelter for the family. Doing all these other things may not have a positive effect if the father feels obligated and performs in a somewhat contrived manner.

Some women feel their breasts swelling and may even produce a drop of milk at the sight of a baby. No physical reaction has been registered for the male; he does not instinctively pick up a baby and hold it. It even has to be explained to him how best to hold such a delicate creature. Many times he feels terrified and will hand the baby over to a woman as soon as possible. Men will proudly show off their son and heir, will buy whatever their children need, but they have to be taught how to hold a bottle of milk to physically feed a baby. This is not to discourage future fathers from sharing all the joy of expecting a child. Maybe if the practice continues to spread, men will become comfortable with it. Some men already are. The question raised here is whether those who are not will somehow disturb the child with a contrived activity. Dr. Sarratt has no answer and neither do I. The maternal instinct and the paternal instinct differ.

What are the husband's obligations toward his wife during her pregnancy? I addressed this question to the religious leaders interviewed for this book. All mentioned kindness, consideration in general terms except for the Buddhist monk from Burma who listed the following specifics advised by the Buddha: There are five obligations a husband has toward his wife and they are: (1) The husband of the pregnant woman must not ignore her; (2) He must give 100% of his earnings into his pregnant wife's hands; (3) He should not desire sexually any woman except his pregnant wife; in fact he must not even comment on the beauty of another woman to her because this might distress her; (4) He must adorn her with all the necessities of life, such as clothing and jewelry; and (5) He must love his pregnant wife with all his capabilities.

Quickening

Speaking of instinct, we sometimes overestimate our sensitivity. Dr. Sarratt tells me that during his examinations he sometimes feels the fetus kicking when the mother had never noticed it herself. After he tells her about it, she will begin to notice it by herself. Just because a fetus kicks does not necessarily mean that he wants further attention from the hand that caresses the abdomen. Often it just kicks to get some exercise or to get out of an uncomfortable position, when the cord gets tangled up.

Natural attachment

What is an uncontestable fact is that once a child is born, all mothers get attached to it. Giving up a child for adoption is extremely hard even when the mother is fully convinced that this is in the best interest of the child. I have dealt with the problems of miscarriage and abortion in the chapter on burial rites. Here I only want to end this book with one piece of solid advice: If you do not want to have a child, do not get pregnant. Use abstinence or birth control.

The last part of the definition of *taikyó*, "to listen to suitable counsel," is exactly what this last chapter wants to accomplish, to know what is best for the mother and the child during pregnancy.

References

Broud, Gwen 1988. "Rethinking the couvade; cross-cultural evidence" *American Anthropologist* vol. 90, No. 4 (December) pp. 902–911.

"Commentaries by Munroe and Broud" (to above) 1989 *American Anthropologist* vol. 91, No. 3 (September) pp. 703–734.

Dikanwa Jiten Showa 61 (3d ed.). Tokyo: Taishukan.

Munroe, Robert L., Ruth Monroe & John W.M. Whiting 1973. "The couvade; a psychological analysis" *Ethos* vol. 1, pp. 30–74.

Nihon Kokuga Daijiten Showa 49. Tokyo: Shogakkan.

Index